MW01003041

West Academic Publishing's Law School Advisory Board

The MPRE

Leah M. Christensen
Associate Professor of Law
Thomas Jefferson School of Law

A SHORT & HAPPY GUIDE® SERIES

WEST
ACADEMIC
PUBLISHING

a short & happy guide series is a trademark registered in the U.S. Patent and Trademark Office.

© 2016 LEG, Inc. d/b/a West Academic

444 Cedar Street, Suite 700
St. Paul, MN 55101
1-877-888-1330

Printed in the United States of America

ISBN: 978-1-63460-347-8

Table of Contents

A Short & Happy Guide to the MPRE

Introduction

You've signed up for the Multi-State Professional Responsibility Exam (MPRE)—so, now what? The MPRE is a sixty-question, 125-minute, multiple-choice examination administered by the National Conference of Bar Examiners. The MPRE is based on the law governing the conduct of lawyers, including the disciplinary rules of professional conduct currently articulated in the ABA Model Rules of Professional Conduct, the ABA Model Code of Judicial Conduct, and controlling constitutional decisions and generally accepted principles established in leading federal and state cases. A passing score on the MPRE is required for admission to the bar in all but four US jurisdictions.

The exam is offered nationwide each Spring, Summer, and Fall, and the majority of states allow students to take the MPRE before graduation from law school. Most students take the exam sometime after their second year of law school. A law school course in ethics is not crucial to your success on the MPRE. Unlike with the bar exam, you can take the MPRE in any state and have your score submitted to another state. In fact, you don't even need to know where you will be taking the bar exam when you take the MPRE. Your score can be transferred at a later date.

The purpose of the MPRE is to measure your knowledge and understanding of established standards related to a lawyer's professional conduct; the MPRE is not a test to determine an individual's personal ethical values. Lawyers serve in many capacities: as judges, advocates, and counselors, and in other roles, too. The law governing the conduct of lawyers in these roles is applied in disciplinary and bar admission procedures, and by courts dealing with issues of appearance, representation, privilege, disqualification, and contempt or other censure.

Many law students assume that they will "know it" when they "see it." In other words, law students think that they will be able to recognize unethical behavior on the MPRE quite easily and, therefore, do not have to study extensively for the MPRE. But the MPRE often tests gray areas—areas where an answer is not necessarily clear. You need to understand the intricacies of the rules.

Further, the MPRE exam is not a law school exam. Studying for the MPRE will be easier than studying for the bar exam or a law school essay exam, but you need to attack the exam efficiently. Too many students fail the MPRE one, two or even three times— because they didn't study effectively. Then test anxiety sets in and it becomes even harder to pass the MPRE.

This Short and Happy Guide is meant to provide you with the essential concepts and overarching themes that you will see tested on the MPRE. The Guide will refer to specific rules throughout. For ease of understanding, we will refer to the rules based upon the Delaware Rules of Professional Conduct, as these rules largely mirror the ABA Model Rules of Professional Conduct. Any reference to a rule number for the Delaware Rules will correspond to the ABA Model Rule number. Consider this Short and Happy Guide to be the best introduction you can have as you begin your exam preparation.

CHAPTER 1

The MPRE Exam and Test Strategies for the MPRE

This chapter will discuss a few unique aspects of the MPRE exam and offer several test strategies to help you navigate successfully through the exam.

To apply for the MPRE, go the website of the National Conference of Bar Examiners, where you can apply easily online. One tip: Think about *where* you want to take the exam. Sometimes, it's nice to take the exam at a location other than your own law school or a school close by. You can avoid some test anxiety by being able to focus on the exam itself, and not the people at the exam whom you know.

A. How Is Your MPRE Score Determined?

Your MPRE score is determined by how many questions you answer correctly; there's no penalty for incorrect answers. The lesson to be learned from this is that it pays to answer *every* question, even if you're not exactly sure what the correct answer is.

5

B. What Is the Scope of the Exam?

Questions about the ABA Model Rules and related sources dealing with the conduct of lawyers and law firms make up about 90-94% of all the questions on the MPRE. The remaining questions test your knowledge of the Model Code of Judicial Conduct.

The NCBE's outline of MPRE subjects, and the approximate weight given to each, is as follows:

1. Regulation of the legal profession (6-12%)

2. The client-lawyer relationship (10-16%)

3. Client confidentiality (6-12%)

4. Conflicts of interest (12-18%), arbitrator, mediator, or other third-party neutral

5. Competence, legal malpractice, and other civil liability (6-12%)

6. Litigation and other forms of advocacy (10-16%)

7. Transactions and communications with persons other than clients (2-8%)

8. Different roles of the lawyer (4-10%)

9. Safekeeping funds and other property (2-8%)

10. Communications about legal services (4-10%)

C. What Are the Questions Like?

Each question contained in the MPRE provides a factual situation along with a specific question or "call" and four possible answer choices. You should choose the best answer from the four stated options and mark only one answer for each question; multiple answers will be scored as incorrect. Since scores are based on the number of questions answered correctly, you should answer every question.

D. How Should You Attack the Fact Patterns?

The fact patterns can be long and very detailed, so you need a plan for how you will attack the fact patterns. You will have about two minutes to read each question, answer it, and move on. This means that you have to have a strong grasp of all of the rules; there's no time to waste trying to remember which rule is which. Further, you have to be able to read through the fact patterns and respond quickly.

To help you do this, you need to teach yourself what to look for. This process is sometimes called finding the "trigger facts," the underlying facts that trigger the legal issues.

Remember that the MPRE is actually very limited in the range of issues it can test. Given that the exam is multiple-choice, the MPRE cannot test gray areas—the facts and rules must point to one and only one correct or best answer. In other words, there cannot be a reasonable argument about which answer is the best answer.

Further, there is a limited number of fact patterns that the examiners can come up with because they are testing not only you, but every other law student in the country, on knowledge of the professional responsibility rules. Therefore, the more you practice, the more you will be able to recognize similar patterns amongst the questions. You really can stick to the main issues of professional responsibility—the MPRE rarely tests obscure issues. In this sense, the MPRE is easier than a typical law school exam.

E.   What Are Important Themes or Statements That You Need to Recognize for the MPRE?

In order to prepare for the MPRE, you need to learn not only the professional responsibility rules, but also how to recognize important themes within the MPRE questions themselves. There are particular statements used in MPRE questions that you will see over and over again, and knowing these statements or patterns will allow to you anticipate correct answer choices more easily. Consider the following pointers:

1.   Pay Attention to Statements About the Lawyer's or the Client's State of Mind

In many of the professional responsibility rules, whether or not a lawyer violates the rule depends upon whether the lawyer *knows or believes* something. The lawyer's knowledge or belief will determine whether some act on his or her part is allowed or disallowed. Note words in a question such as "knows," or "knowingly," or "becomes convinced," or "believes," or "reasonably believes."

For many ethical issues, the attorney's belief about a fact or an event is more important than the fact or event itself. For example, consider a question about a lawyer's role in recommending a candidate for admission to the bar. According to the rules, a lawyer cannot "knowingly" make a false statement of material fact in connection with an applicant's admission to the bar under Rule 8.1.

Looking at the rule carefully, you should notice that it doesn't matter whether the person the lawyer recommends later turns out to be a drug dealer. As long as the lawyer didn't *know* the true facts at the time he or she made the recommendation, he or she will not be subject to discipline.

2. Pay Attention to the Lawyer's Motivation When He or She Acts or Fails to Act

Just as the extent of an attorney's knowledge can affect the propriety or impropriety of his or her behavior, so too can his or her reasons for undertaking or not undertaking a course of action. Take note of the *reason* for an attorney's actions. Often thinking about the reasons related to why a lawyer acted can help you in assessing the propriety of his or her conduct.

3. Pay Attention to the Lawyer's Core Behavior

In some MPRE questions, the examiners test your knowledge of the ethical rules by surrounding unethical behavior with the "window dressings" of proper behavior. This technique tests whether you can identify unethical conduct even when it's surrounded by allegedly "good" behavior. One of the most common ways the examiners try to trick you is by distracting you from the right answer by seeming to "fix" the rule violation with a good outcome or through client consent. Be wary of questions that use this type of fact pattern and answer options.

4. Don't Fall for a Question That Suggests That the Lawyer's Conduct, Though Questionable, Has Not Prejudiced the Client

This is a very common MPRE trap: the facts describe conduct by a lawyer that is wrong, but then tell you that the misconduct has not affected the client. When this happens in an MPRE question, you can bet that at least one of the distractor answers will suggest that the lawyer's conduct was proper because his client was not "prejudiced" or "adversely affected." It's important to keep the following in mind: even if things work out fine for the client, the lawyer may still be subject to discipline for violating the rules in the first place. Once a lawyer has engaged in unethical conduct, it doesn't really matter what the consequence of that conduct is to the client; the lawyer has violated the rules and he or she is subject to discipline.

5. A Client's Insistence on a Course of Conduct Doesn't Relieve the Lawyer of the Responsibility to Follow the Rules

Sometimes an MPRE fact pattern will feature an attorney who has violated the rules at the request of the client. An important rule to remember: the client's insistence on improper conduct by the lawyer does not relieve the lawyer of the obligation not to engage in the conduct.

Knowing these themes will be very helpful in narrowing down the correct answers on the MPRE and eliminating wrong answers.

CHAPTER 2

The Code of Judicial Conduct

It may be surprising to you that the MPRE tests the Model Code of Judicial Conduct. Often in law school Professional Responsibility courses, the class will not have discussed the Code of Judicial Conduct. This Chapter will serve to highlight the most important rules and themes that are tested by the MPRE with regard to judges.

One of the main themes to remember is that judges are held to a higher standard than lawyers. So if a question deals with a judge and a judge's behavior, make sure to analyze the behavior in accordance with the standards for judicial conduct.

Judges play many roles. They interpret the law, assess the evidence presented, and control how hearings and trials unfold in their courtrooms. Most important of all, judges are impartial decision-makers in the pursuit of justice. We have an adversarial system of justice: legal cases are set up as contests between opposing sides, ensuring that evidence and legal arguments will be fully and forcefully presented. The judge, however, must remain above the fray, providing an independent and impartial assessment of the facts and how the law applies to those facts.

A. What Are the Main Ethical Duties of Judges?

Judges are required to uphold the integrity and independence of the judiciary. Further, a judge must avoid the appearance of impropriety in all activities—and the judge is evaluated objectively. Judges must avoid bias, prejudice, and harassment, and they also have a duty to prevent lawyers from engaging in such behaviors.

You may see the phrase "avoid the appearance of impropriety" frequently on the MPRE when discussing the behavior of judges. Here are some specific things that judges must *not* do if they are to maintain propriety. A judge:

1. Cannot voluntarily appear as a character witness.

2. Cannot be a member of discriminatory organizations.

3. Cannot use nonpublic information in judicial decision-making.

4. Cannot practice law while in the position as a judge.

5. Cannot receive compensation for extra-judicial activities.

6. Cannot receive ex parte communications (communications without all parties present), except on non-substantive matters, like scheduling.

So, what *can* judges do that is in accordance with the ethical rules? The next section will go into these issues in more detail.

B. Can Judges Receive Compensation?

Yes, judges can receive limited compensation for judicial activities but they must report all compensation. For example, judges can receive compensation for teaching law classes or lecturing, but the compensation must be reasonable and any reimbursement for expenses must be limited to the actual cost of travel, lodging, etc.

C. Can Judges Hold Outside Positions When Serving as a Judge?

The answer here is also "yes"—for some positions. For example, a judge can serve as an executor, administrator, or other fiduciary, but only if there is a "close familial relationship." However, a judge cannot get involved in matters likely to go to his or her own court.

A judge cannot serve as an arbitrator or practice law while acting as a full-time judge. A judge cannot accept an appointment unless the goal of the organization is to improve the law.

D. Can Judges Participate in Political Activities?

The MPRE loves to test this aspect of the Code of Judicial Conduct. A judge is not allowed to endorse any candidate publicly. When the judge is the person running for office, the judge is permitted to take a position on issues as long as it is done in a dignified way, even on contested political issues. However, a judge is not allowed to personally solicit funds for his or her political campaign—the campaign committee is required to handle all money and public support.

E. How Does a Judge Remain Impartial?

Individual judges must be seen to be objective and impartial. In their personal lives, judges must avoid words, actions, or situations that might make them appear to be biased or disrespectful of the laws they are sworn to uphold. They must treat lawyers, clients, and witnesses with respect and must refrain from comments that suggest they have made up their minds in advance.

Outside the courtroom, judges should not socialize or associate with lawyers or other persons connected with the cases they hear, or they may be accused of bias. Judges typically declare a conflict and withdraw from a case that involves relatives or friends. The same is true if the case involves a former client, a member of the judge's former law firm, and law partners or former business associates, at least until a year or two has passed since the judge was appointed and those ties were severed.

F. When Must a Judge Disqualify Herself?

A judge must disqualify herself where the judge's impartiality might reasonably be questioned. Further, if the judge knows outside facts about the case or knows the lawyers on the case, the judge may need to disqualify herself from the case. Here are some examples of when a judge must disqualify herself from a case:

1. If the judge is biased or prejudiced or has personal knowledge about the facts of a case;

2. If the judge previously served as a lawyer on the case or knows the other lawyers on the case personally; or

3. If the judge, the judge's spouse, or the judge's minor child living in the judge's house has more

than *de minimis* financial or any other interest that could be substantially affected by outcome.

The key to analyzing questions that relate to judicial conduct is to consider an overarching theme: public confidence in the judiciary is promoted by responsible and proper conduct by judges.

In summary, a judge must avoid all impropriety and appearance of impropriety. A judge must expect to be the subject of constant public scrutiny. Judges must therefore accept restrictions on their conduct that might be viewed as burdensome by the ordinary citizen, and they should do so freely and willingly. All of the rules of judicial conduct are for the purpose of maintaining the integrity, impartiality, and independence of the judiciary.

CHAPTER 3

Dishonesty and Misconduct

You may be thinking that it's obvious an attorney should be honest and avoid misconduct. Certainly, this rule will apply to you when you become a lawyer. And in reality, this rule applies to you as soon as you submit your application to sit for any bar exam. If you make a false statement on your bar application or fail to disclose material facts on your bar application, you have violated a lawyer's duty of honesty.

Rule 8.1, which relates to Bar Admission, states that you cannot knowingly make a false statement of material fact or fail to disclose a material fact on your bar application. If you lie on your bar application, you will be subject to discipline after passing the bar.

Now let's look at some of the main issues involving attorney dishonesty and misconduct.

A. What Is the Duty of Honesty?

As an attorney, you are ethically bound by the duty of honesty, which the ethics rules more commonly refer to as the duty of candor. The duty of candor or honesty is found throughout the Rules of Professional Responsibility, and the duty covers everything from client perjury and false evidence to representations about procedural issues and citation of authority in court.

We will talk about each of these individual concepts throughout this book because there is no one rule that fully comprises the duty of candor or honesty. The duty of candor or honesty is found throughout the Rules of Professional Responsibility. As you begin to prepare for the MPRE, it is important to be aware of how honesty and candor come up in numerous ethical rules.

Honesty means being truthful, sincere, upright and fair. Honesty means speaking and writing without spinning the truth, without misrepresenting the truth, and without omitting statements needed to avoid misleading others or embellishing the truth. Opposites of honesty are dishonesty, deceit, and fraud.

The Rules of Professional Responsibility make it clear that the first and highest duty of every lawyer is to be honest. Rule 1.2(d) prohibits lawyers from assisting or counseling a client to engage in criminal or fraudulent conduct. Rule 3.3 provides that a lawyer shall not knowingly make a false statement of fact or law to a tribunal or fail to correct a false statement of material fact or law previously made to the tribunal by the lawyer. Rule 3.3 also prohibits a lawyer from offering evidence the lawyer knows to be false. Rule 3.4(b) provides that a lawyer shall not falsify evidence, or counsel or assist a witness to testify falsely. Rule 4.1 provides that a lawyer shall not knowingly make a false statement of material fact or law to a third person. Rule 7.1 provides that a lawyer shall not make a false or misleading communication about the lawyer or the lawyer's services. A communication is false or misleading if it contains a material misrepresentation of fact or law, or if it omits a fact necessary to make the communication—considered as a whole—not materially misleading.

Rule 8.1 provides that an applicant for admission to the bar shall not knowingly make a false statement of material fact or fail to disclose a fact necessary to correct a misapprehension. Rule 8.2 provides that a lawyer shall not make a statement that the lawyer knows to be false, or with reckless disregard as to its truth or falsity, concerning the qualifications or integrity of a judge.

Rule 8.4 states that it is professional misconduct for a lawyer to commit a criminal act that reflects adversely on the lawyer's honesty, trustworthiness, or fitness as a lawyer, or for a lawyer to engage in conduct involving dishonesty, fraud, deceit, or misrepresentation. A lawyer has a special duty of candor to the courts. The lawyer has an affirmative duty to correct misstatements of fact or law made by the lawyer, even if doing so may hurt the client's position. The lawyer is obligated to correctly characterize the client's position and to correct statements previously made by the lawyer which are not literally true or are materially misleading. Further, a lawyer is required to correct misquoted case law. In no case is the lawyer permitted to offer false evidence or assist or advise the client to testify falsely or assist or counsel a client to commit a crime or fraud.

Pay attention to the duty of candor or honesty as you move through this book, and consider returning to this chapter to review how the duty of candor or honesty manifests itself throughout the rules.

B. What Is Attorney Misconduct?

The main rule covering attorney misconduct is Rule 8.4, which lays out a general duty of honesty and integrity for lawyers. The main idea is that the public should be protected from those who are not qualified to be lawyers. Under the general rule, a lawyer shall not:

1.   Violate the rules of professional conduct or knowingly assist another in such a violation.

2.   Engage in conduct involving dishonesty or moral turpitude. "Moral turpitude" can include any crime committed anywhere that relates to an immoral or bad act. A state can discipline its lawyers for misconduct committed outside the state.

3.   Engage in conduct prejudicial to the administration of justice.

4.   Engage in conduct that adversely reflects on the lawyer's fitness to practice law.

5.   State or imply that the lawyer has the ability to influence the government or a government official.

6.   Knowingly assist a judicial officer in violating the rules of judicial conduct or other law.

One interesting thing to note under the misconduct rule is that the misconduct (or moral turpitude) is covered by the rule regardless of whether the conduct happens as part of a lawyer's practice of law or outside the practice of law. The MPRE loves to test this aspect of the rules: a lawyer violates the misconduct provision even if the misconduct relates to something in the lawyer's personal life.

Moral turpitude can include adultery, possession of child pornography, sexual assault, and comparable offenses, even though these offenses have no specific connection to the fitness to practice law. Offenses involving violence, dishonesty, breach of trust, or serious interference with the administration of justice also fall into the category of moral turpitude.

Further, individual states have very different standards for discipline when it comes to acts of moral turpitude. In some states, a lawyer found to have committed moral turpitude by having more than one DUI (Driving Under the Influence) offense could be disbarred. In another state, a lawyer with multiple DUI's might receive only a suspension.

For the MPRE, pick out trigger facts that point to crimes involving dishonesty, breach of a fiduciary duty, violence, or improper sexual behavior. These types of items are seen frequently on the MPRE and usually relate to an issue involving attorney misconduct under Rule 8.4.

C. What Are a Lawyer's Obligations to Report Misconduct?

Under Rule 8.3, a lawyer who *knows* that another lawyer (or judge) has committed a violation that raises a substantial question as to the person's ability to act as an attorney (or judge) *shall* inform the appropriate authority, unless the information is privileged.

Note a couple of important things about this rule. First, a lawyer must *know* that another lawyer has committed a violation. Having only a suspicion does not rise to the level of requiring the lawyer to report the violation. Second, the conduct must raise a *substantial* question as to the lawyer's fitness to practice law, so there must be a nexus between the conduct and the practice of law. Finally, if another attorney's conduct meets these two criteria, then the lawyer *shall* report the conduct. There are not a lot of places in the ethics rules that require absolutely that a lawyer act. This is one of those places, so pay careful attention to this rule.

D. What if the Misconduct Occurred in State A but the Lawyer Is Licensed in State B?

A lawyer is still subject to discipline even if the lawyer's conduct occurred in a state other than the one in which the lawyer is licensed to practice. Under Rule 8.5, a lawyer is subject to the disciplinary authority of the jurisdiction in which he or she is licensed even when the lawyer is engaged in practice elsewhere. So this means that if you go to Las Vegas and get a DUI—and you go back to California where your practice is located—you can be subject to discipline in California even though the conduct occurred in Nevada.

In summary, misconduct can include a broad range of topics, including both personal and professional misconduct. Attorneys can be disciplined for conduct in their home state even if they've committed the act in another state. But a lawyer need not report misconduct by another attorney unless the lawyer *knows* the other lawyer committed misconduct, and the conduct substantially affects the other lawyer's ability to practice law. The legal profession is a self-regulating profession, but the ethical rules have left lawyers some flexibility about reporting misconduct so we're not constantly turning in our colleagues.

CHAPTER 4

Practicing Without a License and Fee Sharing Among Lawyers

One important concept within the Rules of Professional Responsibility is the notion that you cannot practice law without a license. You might think it would be pretty obvious whether you are or are not *practicing law*. But this issue has actually been highly litigated—it's not nearly as clear as you might think. For example, what if you are working in a law firm in New York, but you have to take depositions of various client employees in California? When you go to California and take those depositions, are you practicing law? The answer is yes, and there's likely an exception that allows this particular activity. But oftentimes there are not exceptions even when you think there would be. So let's address the issue of practicing without a license—a favorite topic of the MPRE.

A. What Is the Practice of Law?

A lawyer is not allowed to practice law in a state without being licensed in that state. What does practicing law mean?

Traditionally, the practice of law is understood to mean work that requires a lawyer's skill and knowledge, and this idea is found in Rule 5.5. Practicing law can simply mean giving legal advice; it also, of course, covers representation in court and other activities.

While historically, the license to practice law must be held in the state where the legal work is being done, there has been a recent trend within the Professional Responsibility Rules to allow something called "multi-jurisdictional practice," which means that lawyers can practice law in a state in which they are not licensed under certain circumstances. The Professional Responsibility Rules have adapted to the practical realities of a modern law practice, with the result that a lawyer working on a case in State A may be allowed to go to State B to interview witnesses (which is practicing law) if the travels are associated with the principal case. Further, a lawyer can apply for *pro hac vice* admission, which is temporary admission for that particular case, by applying to the court where the lawyer needs to appear. As long as the lawyer associates with a locally admitted attorney, judges typically grant *pro hac vice* admissions.

B. Can a Lawyer Accidentally Assist Others in the Practice of Law?

What happens if a busy lawyer has a paralegal prepare discovery documents for a case? Is that improperly assisting another in the practice of law? The answer is: it depends. Under Rule 5.5, it is permissible for a lawyer to delegate work to non-licensed law clerks, assistants, and/or paralegals, provided that all work is adequately supervised by the attorney and the attorney reads every document. The attorney is fully responsible for all such work. If for some reason the attorney does not supervise and/or read the documents, then the attorney has violated this rule.

Rule 5.5 is important to lawyers and law firms for very practical reasons. If a lawyer "practices law" without being licensed in the state, the lawyer could lose any fees that he or she has earned in the case. Several cases have held that if a law firm has allowed its lawyers to practice law in states where they are not licensed, the firm cannot collect any fees related to the work. For some firms in this position, this omission has cost them hundreds of thousands of dollars in fees.

C. Can Lawyers Pay for Referrals from Other Lawyers? Can Lawyers Share Fees with Each Other?

The Rules of Professional Responsibility have generally been grounded in opposition to any commercialization of the act of lawyering, based on the belief that the attorney-client relationship should be completely free of extraneous issues such as financial concerns and/or bias. So the Professional Responsibility Rules tend to place strict limitations on when attorneys may share fees, when attorneys may compensate others for recommending the lawyer's services, and how reciprocal referrals (lawyers referring clients to each other) are to be handled. These rules vary quite dramatically from jurisdiction to jurisdiction, so it is important for both the referring attorney and the accepting attorney to consult the rules of their jurisdiction carefully. For the purposes of the MPRE, you should apply the ABA Model Rules of Professional Responsibility, which are the same as those in the majority of states. This discussion will follow the guidelines of the Delaware Rules, which follow the ABA Model Rules.

Professional Responsibility rules generally prohibit an attorney from paying another attorney to recommend an attorney's services ("referral fees"), unless the attorney meets various exceptions under Rule 7.2. (Note that Rule 7.2 is the rule addressing attorney advertising, which we will discuss in later chapters.) But Rule 7.2 also deals with the issue of whether an attorney can pay another attorney simply for providing a client lead. Generally, the answer is no. However, the MPRE loves to test the exceptions to this rule.

For example, Rule 7.2's proscription against referral fees does not apply to an attorney's normal payments for advertising and communications to "channel" or "refer" work, so long as the advertising and communications otherwise comply with the ethical rules. Further, the referral fee prohibition does not apply to fee sharing, which is another sort of fee arrangement entirely. Fee sharing (sometimes called fee-splitting), where two attorneys from different firms share the representation in a case, is allowed by the ethical rules—as long as the fee division is proportionate to the work performed and/or each attorney assumes joint responsibility, the client agrees to the arrangement in writing, and the total fee is reasonable.

Another exception to the general rule against receiving compensation for referring a client is something called a "reciprocal referral arrangement." Again, this is a favorite concept tested by the MPRE. A reciprocal referral arrangement is where two attorneys agree to mutually refer clients back and forth, for no payment. But the agreement cannot be exclusive. An attorney may enter into a reciprocal referral arrangement with another attorney or a non-attorney professional so long as the arrangement does not violate any other rules, including interference with the an attorney's professional independence. To comply with Rule 7.2 for a reciprocal referral agreement, the agreement must not be exclusive, and the client must be informed of the existence and nature of the agreement.

In addition, an attorney is allowed to pay a legal service plan, a not-for-profit referral service, or qualified lawyer referral service for their services under Rule 7.2. These types of plans are not considered personal attorney advertising or solicitation because the plan providers send out the information to potential clients who then purchase the plan services, as opposed to purchasing the services of a specific lawyer.

D. Can a Lawyer Share Fees with a Non-Lawyer?

Rule 5.4 generally prohibits sharing fees with non-lawyers. This extends to agreements with non-attorneys to solicit clients in return for a share of the fees (i.e., the use of "runners" or "cappers"). This rule again is a favorite issue of the MPRE to test because it may not seem like such a bad thing for a lawyer to collaborate with a non-lawyer. Here's the big problem, however. The Professional Responsibility Rules do not want a non-lawyer to direct or control the professional judgment of a lawyer. Note also that non-lawyers cannot own law firms, and a lawyer cannot form a partnership with any individual not licensed to practice law if any activities of that partnership will be the practice of law. So if your accountant friend wants you to set up a tax practice with her, be careful—you likely cannot undertake that sort of partnership if any of it involves the practice of law.

So watch out for MPRE questions that discuss the unauthorized practice of law by attorneys licensed in one state, but doing some sort of legal work in another state. In addition, watch out for fact patterns that discuss a lawyer sharing fees or getting a portion of a fee just for referring the case. These actions may be violations of the rules discussed above.

CHAPTER 5

Competence, Diligence, and Communication

The main rule of competence is Rule 1.1, which states that a lawyer has a duty to use the legal knowledge, skill, thoroughness, and preparation reasonably necessary for the representation of a client. Perfect competence is not required, but a lawyer cannot be so incompetent that reasonable preparation on a case would not bring him or her up to speed. Lawyers get into trouble with clients and the ethics rules if they take on a case they are incapable of handling, whether it be due to their lack of training or experience, or because the volume of work is simply too much for one person to handle.

For the most part, all of the skills that you learned in law school have general applicability: you've learned how to assess a problem, research the law, and apply law you have discovered to the facts of a case. The rule of competence recognizes that any lawyer can take on a case and understand generally how to research and become competent about the law in that area. However, there are cases and areas of the law that should not be handled by an untrained lawyer. For example, it would be difficult to be ready to defend a client in a murder trial right out of law school.

There are several different factors that a court will examine to determine if a lawyer is acting competently and employing the required knowledge and skill in a particular matter. First, a court will look to the relative complexity and specialized nature of a matter to determine whether a lawyer can competently handle a matter. For example, certain types of law are going to be off-limits to a non-specialist lawyer. One example is patent law. In order to prosecute a patent before the U.S. Patent and Trademark Office ("PTO"), a lawyer must have passed the Patent Bar exam in addition to a state bar exam. Lawyers involved in patent prosecutions often come from scientific backgrounds, which helps in explaining and assessing technical issues. A new lawyer who has no prior knowledge or education in patent law cannot competently represent a client in a patent prosecution.

Courts will also look to the lawyer's experience and training. The rule of competence minimally assumes that each lawyer has the proficiency of a general practitioner. Further, if a lawyer does not have general competence or proficiency in a particular area of law, the court will examine the preparation and study the lawyer needs to accomplish the task. The amount of preparation and study needed to accomplish a task should be reasonable. A lawyer has an obligation to conduct necessary legal research and also must investigate all facts that are relevant to a case. However, a lawyer cannot pass along to the client the cost of the lawyer's time and energy spent in gaining competence.

Consider the following example: A corporate lawyer takes on a DUI case for a friend of his son's. The lawyer has never done this kind of criminal work before but wants to help his son's friend. The corporate lawyer researches a great deal and works very hard on the case. The lawyer wants the client to win so that the young man's police record will remain unblemished.

The client prevails, and he and his attorney are ecstatic. One problem—the lawyer charges by the hour, at $450 an hour. The client is left with a legal bill of $40,000 when the case could have been competently handled by an experienced criminal defense attorney for a fraction of that cost. Did the lawyer act competently? Will the lawyer be paid for all of his fees?

Here, the lawyer did act competently. Through research and effort, the lawyer learned the law in that area well enough to be able to properly defend the case and be successful on his client's behalf. However, the lawyer will not be able to recover the high attorney's fees because the client is not required to pay for a lawyer to become competent. The lawyer will need to reduce his fees to the average amount an attorney would charge to defend a DUI case.

Finally, in addition to the above, in determining competence, a court will examine whether it is feasible for the attorney to consult with another lawyer who is established in the related field. If a lawyer does not have competence in a particular area, a lawyer can associate with another lawyer to gain competence. Lawyers of all types must be willing to admit if the skills they possess are inadequate for the task at hand. It would be unethical for a lawyer to collect a fee in a case knowing the lawyer will not be able to handle the case with competence.

There's an important exception to Rule 1.1 called the "emergency exception." In an emergency where referral to or consultation or association with another lawyer would be impractical, a lawyer may give advice or assistance in a matter in which the lawyer does not have the skill ordinarily required. Consider this example. A new lawyer is working late one evening at his firm. The lawyer receives a call from his cousin who is currently in jail after getting into bar fight. The cousin asks the lawyer to post bail and get him out of jail. The new lawyer's experience with criminal law is limited to what he learned in his criminal law class during his first year of law school. The lawyer tells his cousin that he is not qualified to help him but his cousin pleads with him and eventually the new lawyer agrees to help. The new lawyer goes to the jail and attempts to negotiate and post bail for his cousin but is unsuccessful. Immediately the next morning, the new lawyer calls a criminal lawyer who gets his cousin out of jail within an hour. Did the new lawyer breach the duty of competence?

The answer is no. The attorney did not breach the duty of competence because his actions fell within the emergency exception. In an emergency, a lawyer is permitted to provide assistance to a client even if it is beyond the lawyer's typical practice area as long as the lawyer does not take the representation farther than necessary to remedy the emergency situation. In the present case, it was late at night and the lawyer could not associate or refer his cousin to an attorney with more experience. The new lawyer did the best he could under the circumstances and immediately referred the case as soon as practicable. If instead, the new lawyer had continued to represent his cousin in the criminal matter without referring the case to another lawyer or associating with another lawyer, he might have breached the duty of competence. In an emergency, assistance should be limited to that reasonably necessary in the circumstance; continuing the case after the emergency could jeopardize the client's interest.

A. What Is the Rule of Diligence?

In conjunction with the lawyer's duty of competence is the lawyer's duty of diligence. Under Rule 1.3, a lawyer shall act with reasonable diligence and promptness in representing a client. Practicing lawyers are busy people and can get into trouble if they procrastinate. Cases rarely go smoothly, and there are always innumerable tasks to accomplish, including papers to fill out and file, documents to draft, calls to make, and meetings to schedule. A setback in the form of a forgotten document filing could easily cause harm to a client's case. This all goes to show that a lawyer must be diligent and organized throughout the entirety of the case.

Consider the following example. Your neighbor comes up to you as you're getting your mail. She explains a legal problem to you in a long, drawn-out story. You're going through the stack of bills from your mailbox. You listen with half an ear and tell her you know just the attorney who can help her with her problem. You tell her that you'll put her in touch with the other attorney. You part ways and you go off to work, but you forget to write down a reminder about this woman's case and what you said you'd do.

A few months later, the neighbor sees you again and tells you that she just went to another lawyer, who told her she can no longer file her case because the statute of limitations ran on the case the week before. Have you violated the duty of diligence to your neighbor?

Possibly. If a court determines that you assumed some professional responsibility for the matter, which is based upon whether you had established an attorney-client relationship with your neighbor, you could be found to have violated the duty of diligence to your neighbor by assuming a responsibility but not following through with it. A court might hold that your obligation to the woman is more than a simple courtesy if she believed you were her attorney.

B. What Is the Duty to Communicate?

A lawyer has a responsibility to communicate with their clients. Rule 1.4 requires that a lawyer must keep a client reasonably informed about the status of a case. The lawyer must promptly comply with reasonable requests for information. The lawyer also must explain a matter to the extent reasonably necessary to permit the client to make informed decisions in the case.

Lawyers are notorious for not returning phone calls. For a litigator who spends most of the work day going in and out of the courtroom, this is understandable. But a good litigator will get in touch with a client as soon as possible to let the client know that it may take a day to call back.

There are certain things that lawyers *must* communicate to their clients. For example, a lawyer must communicate all offers of settlement made by opposing parties. A lawyer must also respond to a client request for information in a reasonable amount of time. Lawyers failing to communicate with their clients is one of the most frequent complaints that clients have about their lawyers. By failing to communicate, you set yourself up to be the target of a malpractice complaint. The MPRE recognizes the frequency of this problem, so you will see several questions on any MPRE that deal with competency, diligence or communication.

CHAPTER 6

Client Trust Accounts

It may be surprising to you as a law student, but you need to start learning and thinking about client trust accounts—and how you will handle your client's money. This is an area that leads to a number of ethical issues for new lawyers, so you will always find at least a couple of questions on the MPRE pertaining to client trust accounts.

Here's the basic rule under Rule 1.15. When a lawyer is in possession of a client's funds, the lawyer owes the client a fiduciary duty to protect, safeguard, and segregate this money from the lawyer's own personal business accounts. As every lawyer knows, a fiduciary is a trustee with scrupulous obligations of trust, good faith, and candor.

When you are a practicing attorney, you will always have two bank accounts: (1) an account for your business funds and any amount of fees that you have earned; and (2) a client trust account where only client money (including unearned fees or retainers) is deposited. The key is that the two types of monies must never be commingled, and it is this concept—i.e., no commingling—that is tested most heavily on the MPRE.

A.　What Is a Client Trust Account?

A client trust account is a checking account that is established by the lawyer to hold a client's money. Depending on the particular lawyer's needs, a lawyer may have a single account to hold all clients' money, or several accounts. However, all such accounts must be maintained separately from the lawyer's own personal funds and other operating business accounts. Funds that are to be shared by the lawyer and the client should be placed into the client trust account until earned. Thus, legal fees which are advanced (typically referred to as "retainers") usually should be deposited and kept in the client trust account until the fee is earned. Some advanced fees or retainers can go into the lawyer's business account, but only if the retainer is non-refundable (see below regarding "advanced fees.")

The purpose of a lawyer trust account is to safeguard the lawyer from the commingling of funds and to prevent the appearance of improper behavior of the lawyer. The account also provides a recordkeeping trail of all payments made from client funds.

Client trust accounts must be maintained in a federally insured financial institution located in the state where the lawyer's office is located. They may be kept in a separate account elsewhere only with the consent of the client. A favorite MPRE question is a fact pattern where the lawyer's office is in State A but the trust account is in State B. Typically, this is impermissible under Rule 1.15 unless there is specific client consent—so watch out for this question.

Further, all client funds must be kept in an interest-bearing account at the federally insured institution. All interest from pooled trust accounts must be deposited with the *Interest on Lawyer Trust Account* (IOLTA) program. Rule 1.15(f) establishes how the IOLTA money is used; in most states, it is usually given to the state bar programs to help with free legal service programs. Note: a lawyer must never retain the interest on a lawyer trust account. A lawyer's fiduciary duty prohibits such retention.

B. Where Are Advanced Legal Fees Kept?

The answer to this question really depends upon the fee agreement with the client. If the money is due and owing to the lawyer at the time of payment, the money should be deposited into the lawyer's operating account. However, if the money must still be earned, the money remains the client's and the money must be placed into the lawyer's trust account.

Note that under Rule 1.16, Termination of Representation, a lawyer has an obligation to refund unearned legal fees to a client when the lawyer's assignment is completed or when the lawyer withdraws or is discharged from employment.

Expenses advanced for litigation are treated similarly to advanced legal fees. How the money is kept depends upon the fee agreement between the lawyer and the client and whether the money is to remain the client's property until payment is required for a specific litigation expense or court fee. If indeed the money is to remain the client's property, the money must be deposited into the lawyer trust account and segregated from the lawyer's personal funds.

C. What if There Is a Dispute About the Distribution of the Money by a Client?

This is a favorite question of the MPRE: when a client disputes your attorney's fee, what do you with the monies you may have in your account that the client already paid? If a client is disputing all or part of a lawyer's fee, the lawyer must retain the disputed funds in the client trust account and move any undisputed portion to the lawyer's operating and/or business account. Note that you cannot leave undisputed fees in your client trust account—you've earned those fees and they need to be in your account and not the client's account. This concept is always tested on the MPRE.

As an example, let's assume a lawyer submitted a bill to the client for $2000. The client had previously provided a retainer in the amount of $2000. However, the client calls and questions the bill, stating that she (the client) believes the bill should only be $1500. In this situation, the lawyer is required to put the $1500 earned fees into the lawyer's business account because the fees have been earned and there is no dispute about the $1500 in fees. However, the lawyer must leave the $500 that is in dispute in the client trust account—even if the lawyer believes that her fees are justified.

In summary, if the client disputes any amount of the fees, that disputed amount must be left in the client trust account but the undisputed amount should be placed in the lawyer's business account. Note, too, that the lawyer must then attempt to promptly resolve the fee dispute with the client. If you understand these basic concepts surrounding client trust accounts, you will get the MPRE questions on this topic correct—which is a great way to work towards a passing score.

CHAPTER 7

Lawyer Advertising and Solicitation

Lawyers are subject to some of the strictest marketing and advertising rules of any profession, and the rules have become even more complicated lately with the explosion of attorneys' use of online marketing.

Attorneys have been permitted to advertise since the U.S. Supreme Court held in 1977 that First Amendment free speech protection extends to commercial speech and applies to attorneys. *Bates v. State Bar of Ariz.*, 433 U.S. 350 (1977). Unlike fully protected "core" or "political" speech, however, the right of attorneys to advertise is subject to regulation and limitation. In general, courts have held that states and the federal government are free to prevent the dissemination of commercial speech that is false, deceptive, or misleading. These terms are at the core of Professional Responsibility Rules concerning advertising: attorneys can advertise as long as the advertisements are not false, deceptive, or misleading.

The attorney advertising rules may at first seem complex, but they come down to three main requirements for any form of lawyer advertising that you should keep in mind for the MPRE. Advertising must:

1. Be truthful (i.e., factual and not misleading);

2. Be labeled as "Attorney Advertising" on the appropriate document or website; and

3. Carry any necessary disclaimers (e.g., specializations).

The next section of this chapter will go through the main ethical rules governing attorney advertising and solicitation.

The main rule governing attorney advertising and solicitation is Rule 7.1, which states that an attorney communication cannot be false or misleading. Most of the MPRE questions relating to advertising deal with this rule. Your job with an advertising MPRE question is to assess if the ad violates Rule 7.1 by determining whether any statements made in the communication are false or misleading. Note that "communication" is broadly interpreted: it can be a paper ad, a letter, a phone call, a website, or even, potentially, an attorney's blog.

Rule 7.2 lays out the guidelines for the public dissemination of information about the lawyer. The rule recognizes that attorneys are allowed to advertise their services. Specifically, the rule allows public dissemination of information concerning a lawyer's name or firm name, address, email address, website, and telephone number. An attorney may also advertise the kinds of services the lawyer will undertake, the fees for those services, the lawyer's foreign language ability (if any), and client testimonials, including their names, as long as the clients have consented to have their information made public.

Note that each state jurisdiction may have slightly different rules regarding advertising. Some jurisdictions have strong prohibitions against "undignified" advertising, such as those late-night television ads where attorneys are doing and saying outrageous things with the hope of getting clients.

One other important aspect of Rule 7.2 is that it prohibits "referral fees": paying others to recommend a lawyer's services. Many law students assume that referral fees are permissible. But it is important to remember that they actually are not allowed under most states' rules—with a couple of limited exceptions. An attorney is generally allowed to pay advertising costs incurred by using marketing or client development services. In addition, a lawyer can pay the usual charges to a legal services plan or a non-profit lawyer referral service. A legal service plan is a prepaid or group legal service plan that helps people who want legal representation. Often people will pay a monthly fee to become a member of such a service. A lawyer referral service, on the other hand, is any organization that holds itself out to the public as a lawyer referral service. Such referral services are supposed to provide unbiased referrals to lawyers with appropriate experience in the subject matter of the representation. These types of referral services must be approved by the state bar of an attorney's state, so these services are highly regulated.

There's one additional and important exception: a lawyer may agree to refer clients to another lawyer, or a non-lawyer professional, in return for that second person agreeing to refer clients or customers to the lawyer. This arrangement is called a reciprocal referral arrangement. Note that no money is involved. This type of arrangement is acceptable as long as it does not interfere with the lawyer's professional judgment about making referrals or about providing substantive legal services.

A. Can a Lawyer Directly Solicit a Client?

The general answer is no. Rule 7.3 addresses the direct solicitation of clients. A lawyer cannot solicit professional employment by in-person, live telephone, or real-time electronic contact if the attorney is seeking to make money from the services (as opposed to offering pro bono services). There are three exceptions to the prohibition on direct solicitation of clients, and you need to know these for the MPRE: you can use direct solicitation if the potential client is a lawyer, a family member, or someone with whom the lawyer had a prior professional relationship. For the purposes of the MPRE, you should start with the presumption that direct solicitation of clients is not generally permitted and then look for any exceptions.

Rule 7.3 has a couple of additional requirements that the MPRE likes to test: first, every advertisement or solicitation must contain the words "Advertising Material." A typical MPRE question will provide you with an advertisement and ask you if it is acceptable under the rules. You may be focusing on whether the ad is misleading, but do not forget to see if the advertisement has the required disclaimer: "Advertising Material." Second, remember that Rule 7.2 allows a lawyer to participate in a prepaid group legal service plan. Under Rule 7.3, the plan is permitted to use in-person or telephone contact to solicit memberships. The rules allow solicitation in this situation because it's not the lawyer making the direct solicitation to the potential client. Instead, the call is being made by an unbiased group legal service plan. So there's less of a chance for overreaching or harassment of any potential clients.

B. Can Lawyers Advertise That They Are Experts in Their Field?

Possibly. Rule 7.4 deals with discussing the "specialties" of lawyers. Neither a lawyer nor a law firm may claim that the lawyer or law firm is a specialist or specializes in a particular area of law, except that: (1) a lawyer admitted to engage in patent practice may use the designation "Patent Attorney;" and (2) a lawyer who is certified as a specialist in a particular area of law or practice by a private organization approved for that purpose (e.g., the American Bar Association) may state that certification if the certifying organization is identified. On the MPRE, watch out for questions about an advertisement in which an attorney is listed as a specialist. Make sure that there's a qualifying certification explaining the source of the specialization and you'll get this question correct.

Finally, Rule 7.5 addresses law firm names (and the use of trade names and the like). The MPRE loves to test this specific rule as well. A lawyer cannot use a firm name, letterhead, or other professional designation that is in any way misleading, or one that suggests a connection to a government agency or charitable legal services organization. An example that violates this rule is to name your law firm "Legal Services Organization, LLC.," because this implies that you are a non-profit, governmental legal services law firm. Further, on letterhead, if a law firm has offices in several jurisdictions, Rule 7.5 requires that the letterhead identify in which jurisdiction(s) each of the lawyers is licensed to practice to avoid any confusion. Finally, lawyers cannot state or imply that they practice in a partnership if they are not legally partners. So, for example, if lawyers are only office-sharing, the lawyers cannot suggest or imply that they are in a legal partnership.

Now let's move to some specific issues under lawyer advertising and solicitation. These areas are ripe for testing on the MPRE because they deal with the more practical realities of online lawyer advertising.

C. Is an Attorney's Website Considered Lawyer Advertising Under the Ethics Rules?

The answer is a definite "yes." A website is a communication about a lawyer's services and often contain claims, areas of expertise, and/or solicitations for employment. All of the advertising rules discussed above apply to an attorney's website, and there are a few areas in particular where it's easy to run afoul of the ethics rules.

To start, the prohibition in Rule 7.1 against false or misleading communication means that trade names, slogans, and even a lawyer's website's URL cannot contain unsubstantiated "marketing speak." This means that a lawyer cannot call herself "San Diego's Winningest Personal Injury Lawyer" unless the lawyer provides hard facts to back that up. Further, an attorney cannot use www.patent.law-god.com as the website URL.

Further, the website must contain the disclaimer that it is "Attorney Advertising," just as is required for paper/written attorney advertising by Rule 7.3.

What about sending emails to prospective clients? Under Rule 7.3, even emails must contain the "Advertising Material" disclaimer at both the beginning and end of the emails, especially if those emails are sent to prospective clients known to be in need of legal services in a particular matter, such as victims of an accident. Note that Rule 7.3 typically does not apply to email messages sent to other lawyers, close friends and family, or an attorney's existing client base.

Finally, your website and emails should contain a disclaimer that you are providing legal information, not advice. If potential clients have the ability to contact you through your website (such as through a contact form), you should make it clear that the use of your website does not create an attorney-client relationship, so no confidential information should be sent. Finally, if you talk about case outcomes in your marketing, you should let the reader know that no results are guaranteed, and that they will vary depending on the case.

D. Can a Lawyer Discuss Past Cases?

The MPRE has frequently tested this issue. The answer is "yes," an attorney can discuss past cases, but the golden rule is to get the client's permission first.

This issue involves not only the advertising rules for attorneys, but also the duty of confidentiality. Under Rule 1.6, a lawyer cannot reveal information relating to the representation of a client unless the client gives informed consent. This rule applies to both current and past clients, so a lawyer can only discuss the results of a past case with client consent.

E. Is a Blog Subject to the Rules Regulating Attorney Advertising?

The answer is potentially yes, but only if the blog post written by the attorney relates directly or obviously to the attorney's availability for employment. Therefore, a blog on an attorney or law firm's professional website likely will be found to be advertising, just as the website itself is advertising. An attorney's professional website is a "communication" within the meaning of Rule 7.1, and this conclusion is not altered by the inclusion in the website of information of general public interest. These conditions also apply to information of a general nature contained on the website, such as articles, information provided in a narrative form, and FAQ's (frequently asked questions) provided by the attorney to assist the public in understanding the law.

Attorneys have been disciplined for blog posts that have focused on an attorney's courtroom or professional successes *and* created a false impression that the attorney can achieve the same results for the reader. The rationale is that even a truthful report of a lawyer's achievements for clients may still be misleading if presented so that a reasonable person could expect that the same results could be obtained in similar matters without regard for the specific factual and legal circumstances of each situation. In other words, even a truthful statement can be found to violate the rules if it is misleading—this concept is important, and the MPRE tests it frequently. So your analysis for any advertising issue should include not only whether the statement is false or deceptive, but also whether the statement—even if true—could be misleading to a potential client. Therefore, a blog or other advertisement should have, at a minimum, a disclaimer to the effect that each case is different and that prior results are no guarantee of future success. This requirement applies to client endorsements and testimonials as well. While such statements presumptively violate the rule, that presumption may be overcome through a disclaimer.

In summary, the key to applying the attorney advertising rules is to make sure that a communication is truthful and not misleading, that the communication is labeled properly as "Attorney Advertising," and that any firm letterhead or website lists all certifications and jurisdictions in which all attorneys are licensed specifically. By keeping in mind these rules, you will navigate successfully through the attorney advertising questions on the MPRE.

CHAPTER 8

Attorney's Fees

This chapter will focus on the issue of attorney's fees, which is one of the most important and testable issues on the MPRE. Rule 1.5 governs the ethical issues involved with attorney's fees. In summary, an attorney should always document the fee arrangement with a client in an attorney-client agreement. In particular, the lawyer must set forth the scope of the representation (i.e., what the lawyer will do for the client), the basis or rate of the attorney's fee, and the expenses for which the client will be responsible. Each of these things must be communicated to the client before or within a reasonable time after commencing the representation. The only exception to this requirement is when the lawyer charges a regularly-represented client on the same basis or rate as in the past.

There are several different types of fees that a lawyer can charge, but the most common fee types are an hourly charge, a flat fee, or a percentage of the amount recovered (often called a "contingency fee").

In setting the basis or rate of the fee, a lawyer must comply with Rule 1.5, which prohibits a lawyer from charging or collecting an unreasonable fee or an unreasonable amount for expenses. The key to Rule 1.5 is the term *unreasonable*. The rule provides various factors that a court will consider in determining the reasonableness of the fee, and you will apply these factors on the MPRE when you are evaluating a fee question. The factors for reasonableness include the following:

1. the time and labor required, the novelty and difficulty of the questions involved, and the skill required to perform the legal service properly;

2. the likelihood, if apparent to the client, that the acceptance of the particular employment will preclude other employment by the lawyer;

3. the fee customarily charged in the locality for similar legal services;

4. the amount involved and the results obtained;

5. the time limitations imposed by the client or by the circumstances;

6. the nature and length of the professional relationship with the client;

7. the experience, reputation, and ability of the lawyer or lawyers performing the services; and

8. whether the fee is fixed or contingent.

An overarching theme to Rule 1.5 is that a lawyer should not exploit any fee arrangement with a client, particularly when an attorney charges an hourly fee. For example, a lawyer cannot bump up their fees by purposefully using inefficient procedures. Courts scrutinize fee agreements to make sure that the fees are reasonable and that the fees were not inflated. In any fee question on the MPRE, you want to first consider the issue of the reasonableness of fees. But note: just because a fee received by an attorney is a large amount does not necessarily mean that the fee is unreasonable. Consider all the factors above to come to that determination.

Let's look at some other common MPRE issues involving attorney's fees.

A. Does a Fee Agreement Always Need to Be in Writing?

The answer here is: it depends. Specifically, the answer depends on whether the fee agreement involves a contingent fee (writing required) or some arrangement other than a contingent fee agreement (no writing required).

If the fee agreement does not involve a contingent fee, then a writing is not required (although as a practical matter, you should always reduce an agreement to writing). When a lawyer intends to charge a client a contingent fee, a contingent fee agreement must be in writing signed by the client. Further, Rule 1.5 requires that the fee agreement be very clear on various items in the fee arrangement, including:

1. the method by which the fee is to be determined, including the percentage or percentages that shall accrue to the lawyer in the event of settlement, trial, or appeal;

2. all the litigation and other expenses to be deducted from the recovery; and

3. whether such expenses are to be deducted before or after the contingent fee is calculated.

A contingent fee agreement must also clearly notify the client of any expenses for which the client will be liable whether or not the client is the prevailing party. When the contingent fee matter is concluded, Rule 1.5 requires the lawyer to provide the client with a written statement stating the outcome of the matter, and if there is a recovery, showing the remittance to the client and the method of its determination.

Note that Rule 1.5 also prohibits a lawyer from entering into a contingent fee agreement in certain types of actions affecting the family (divorce cases) or when representing a defendant in a criminal case or any proceeding that could potentially result in jail time.

As noted above, there is one exception to the writing requirement in a contingent fee agreement: a lawyer does *not* have to communicate with the client about the scope of the representation, or the basis or rate of the fee and the expenses for which the client is responsible, if the lawyer will be charging a regularly-represented client on the same basis or rate as in the past. What is a regularly-represented client? The rules do not define the phrase. However, when the lawyer has regularly represented a client, the lawyer and client ordinarily will have an understanding between them concerning the basis or rate of the fee and the expenses for which the client will be responsible. This analysis suggests that sporadic or infrequent representation is unlikely to have produced such an understanding and would not constitute regular representation.

B. When Does a Lawyer Need to Talk to the Client About Fees?

Rule 1.5 requires that the communication concerning the scope of the representation, the basis or rate of the fee, and the expenses for which the client will be responsible be communicated to the client before or within a *reasonable time* after commencing the representation. A lawyer accordingly may start working for the client without such a communication as long as the client is provided with the written communication concerning fees within a reasonable time thereafter. What constitutes a reasonable amount of time after the representation has begun? The answer will depend upon the circumstances. Rule 1.5 contemplates that the client be advised of important information concerning the representation before the matter proceeds very far so that the client is not inconvenienced unnecessarily if the client decides to hire a different lawyer after considering the information. Therefore, the communication should be done as soon as reasonably practical.

C. What Constitutes a "Writing"? Does It Always Have to Be a Formal Document?

No, a formal document is not required by the rules. A writing could be something as simple as an email, a letter or memorandum, or a copy of the lawyer's customary fee arrangements.

D. What if the Lawyer Changes the Fee During the Course of the Representation?

Rule 1.5 requires that any changes in the basis or rate of the fee or expenses be communicated to the client in writing. There are no exceptions to this requirement. Thus, even in the case of a regularly-represented client as to whom no communication regarding fees and expenses was initially required, information concerning a change in the basis or rate of the fee (for example, an increase in hourly rates) must be communicated to the client in writing. A change in rates does not necessarily require a separate written notification to the client, but it does require at least a clear statement on a bill sent to the client notifying the client of the change and indicating the new basis or rate of the fee or expenses.

E. Can a Lawyer Charge a Client for the Typical Expenses of Taking a Case to Trial?

The answer is yes. An attorney can pass along reasonable expenses to the client. However, a client must be informed ahead of time about those expenses for which the client will be responsible. If the client will be charged for photocopying costs, court reporter fees, filing fees, and the like, the lawyer must communicate that fact at the outset of the representation. Rule 1.5 does not require that the fee agreement state the specific amount of the costs that will be charged to the client (for example, the per-page cost for photocopying), but a lawyer should try to provide that information to the client if known.

One important limit, however, is that a lawyer cannot collect an unreasonable amount of money for expenses. A lawyer may seek reimbursement for the actual cost of services performed in-house, such as copying, or for other expenses incurred in-house, such as telephone charges. However, a lawyer cannot artificially inflate such expenses to make a profit.

F. Are Retainer Fees Covered by Rule 1.5?

The answer is yes. Retainer fees are an amount paid to a lawyer in contemplation of future services; they can be earned at an agreed-upon basis, whether hourly, flat, or in another way. Any amount paid to a lawyer in contemplation of future services, whether on an hourly, flat or other basis, is an advanced fee— regardless of whether that fee is characterized as an 'advanced fee,' 'minimum fee,' 'nonrefundable fee,' or otherwise. In other words, all advanced fees are subject to the requirements of fee agreements. In the fee agreement, the lawyer should identify whether any portion of the fee is an advanced or retainer fee, and if so, what portion of the fee is a retainer.

G. Does a Client Have to Sign the Agreement for the Agreement Be Valid?

Rule 1.5 does not require the client's signature on a writing that communicates the information required by Rule 1.5 (i.e., the scope of the representation and the basis or rate of the fee and expenses for which the client will be responsible). Contingent fee agreements, however, must be signed by the client. A writing signed by the client also is required in certain situations involving a division of fees between lawyers who are not in the same firm (split-fee arrangements).

Remember that a division of fee between lawyers who are not in the same firm may be made only if: (1) the client consents to employment of the other lawyer after a full disclosure that a division of fees will be made; (2) the division is made in reasonable proportion to the services performed or responsibility or risks assumed by each; and (3) the total fee of the lawyers is reasonable.

H. What if a Client Disputes the Attorney's Fees?

When a lawyer and client have become involved in a dispute over fees, the lawyer must proceed with caution. It is quite possible that a fee dispute with a client could lead to a conflict of interest. We will discuss this issue in detail in a later chapter involving conflicts of interest, but we will touch on Rule 1.7, the general conflict of interest rule, here because it can apply in fee dispute situations. Rule 1.7 states that a lawyer shall not represent a client if the representation will be materially limited by a personal interest of the lawyer. If there is such a personal limitation, i.e., a lawyer is attempting to collect a fee from the client, then it's possible a conflict exists. At that point, the lawyer would need the consent of the client and a waiver from the client to proceed (which may be difficult to get). If the lawyer cannot get a waiver from the client, then it's quite possible that a lawyer must withdraw at this point because continuing the representation would result in a violation of the Rules of Professional Responsibility or other law. In sum, if the fee dispute has made it impossible for the lawyer to place the client's interests ahead of his or her own, a conflict exists and the lawyer should move to withdraw.

I. What About Disputed Fees and the Client Trust Account?

One important issue that is tested by the MPRE is whether disputed fees have to be left in the Client Trust Account. The answer is yes. Any disputed amount must be left in the Client Trust Account and should not be placed in the lawyer's business account unless and until the fee dispute is resolved in favor of the amount moved to the business account.

Thus, if a client is disputing all or part of the lawyer's fee, the lawyer must retain the disputed funds in the Client Trust Account and move any undisputed portion to the lawyer's operating account. However, the lawyer may not simply allow the disputed funds to remain in the trust account indefinitely. The lawyer must attempt a prompt resolution of the fee dispute with the client. Several methods of resolution are possible. First, the lawyer may directly negotiate the fee dispute with the client. Second, most states offer a fee arbitration program aimed at resolving such disputes. Finally, the lawyer may consider the possibility of depositing the property or funds in dispute into the registry of the applicable court so that the matter may be adjudicated.

J. Can a Lawyer Charge Interest on the Outstanding Balance of Fees?

The answer is yes. Nothing in the rules prohibits a lawyer from charging a reasonable rate of interest on outstanding balances that the client owes to the attorney. However, if the lawyer intends to charge interest on unpaid balances, that information must be in the attorney-client engagement letter. A lawyer who adds interest charges without any prior notification to the client runs the risk of violating Rule 1.5, which requires that the lawyer communicate about the basis or rate of the fee.

In summary, a good working relationship with a client requires proper communication concerning the fees and expenses for which the client will be responsible. Rule 1.5 is designed to ensure that this communication occurs. If there is a dispute about the attorney's fees, the disputed funds should be left in the trust account. You cannot bring a claim against your client to recover your fees until your work for the client has concluded.

CHAPTER 9

Limitations on the Right to Practice and Sale of a Law Practice

In the business world, it's not uncommon for a business professional to enter into an agreement that restricts the right of the professional to compete, and such restrictions can be enforced if the restriction is reasonable. These types of agreements are often called non-compete agreements.

Lawyers have a very different rule that applies to them. Rule 5.6 prohibits a lawyer from participating in any partnership, shareholder, operating, employment, or other type of agreement that restricts a lawyer's right to practice. In other words, a lawyer cannot participate in offering or making a partnership or employment agreement that restricts the rights of a lawyer to practice after termination of the relationship. A lawyer who participates in such an agreement is subject to discipline. The policy behind the rule is a concern for both lawyers and clients. The concern for lawyers is that restrictive agreements limit a lawyer's freedom to practice law. The concern for clients is that these agreements limit a client's ability to have their counsel of choice. The one exception, discussed below, concerns retirement benefits.

A. Are Non-Compete Agreements Enforceable?

Probably not. Courts are reluctant to enforce any agreement that restricts a lawyer's right to practice (a non-compete agreement) because these agreements do violate the rules of professional responsibility for lawyers and, therefore, contradict public policy. When the agreement directly restricts competition, then courts will not likely enforce the agreement. Most courts also refuse to enforce agreements that do not restrict competition per se, but do restrict a lawyer indirectly by imposing financial disincentives or by providing penalties for competition. A few courts have enforced contracts with financial disincentives to competition, but they evaluate the restrictions on competition using a reasonableness standard.

B. What Is the Retirement Exception?

As mentioned above, Rule 5.6 prohibits restrictions on a lawyer's right to practice. There is an exception, however, called the Retirement Exception. If the restriction on the right to practice law is part of an agreement regarding retirement benefits, the restriction may be permissible. The rationale for the exception is that a retiring lawyer would not be available for clients anyway, so restricting that lawyer's right to practice would really have no practical effect on the lawyer or on the client population.

How do you determine whether an agreement actually relates to retirement benefits? An agreement or a provision of an agreement does *not* relate to retirement benefits (and is not within the exception) unless the provision affects benefits available only to lawyers retiring from the practice of law.

Further, to be considered a provision relating to retirement benefits, the provision cannot penalize a lawyer by taking away funds already earned. Other indicators that are not necessarily outcome-determinative of a retirement benefit arrangement include benefit calculation formulas.

C. What Type of Restrictive Agreements Are Improper?

Agreements that restrict a lawyer's right to practice by prohibiting that lawyer from representing other clients in claims against the original adverse party are viewed as improper. For example, as part of a settlement agreement in a tobacco lawsuit, the plaintiff's lawyer could not enter into an agreement, as a condition to settling the current lawsuit, that the lawyer would not represent any plaintiffs in future tobacco lawsuits. Why would the defense in our example want this provision in the settlement agreement? If plaintiff's attorney was, for example, extremely proficient at litigating these types of cases, the defense might want to prevent the attorney from filing future suits on behalf of other clients. Rule 5.6 prevents this type of restriction from occurring.

D. Can a Lawyer Sell a Law Practice?

Yes, a lawyer can sell a law practice as long as the lawyer complies with various procedural and ethical rules embodied in Rule 1.17. But the lawyer cannot sell a law practice unless the lawyer is leaving the private practice of law completely, is leaving the private practice of law in a particular jurisdiction or geographic area, or no longer plans to practice the type of practice the lawyer is selling.

Let's face it. The practice of law can be grueling at times. A lawyer might want to leave the private practice of law to retire entirely, to become a judge, or to become an in-house lawyer for a corporation, for example. If a lawyer wants to sell her practice to retire, Rule 1.17 allows the lawyer to sell an entire practice to another lawyer. A lawyer may also sell her practice even if she plans to practice in another jurisdiction. And a lawyer may sell the entire practice or a subject area of the practice—as long as the lawyer sells the entire subject area. For example, let's say a lawyer no longer wants to practice in family law—at all. The lawyer can sell this subject area of the practice.

A lawyer cannot, however, sell certain cases while keeping others of the same kind. Perhaps a lawyer's practice neatly divides into personal injury cases and divorce cases. If the lawyer is leaving the practice of law, the lawyer may sell her entire practice to another lawyer, Lawyer 2. Perhaps that Lawyer 2 specializes in personal injury representation. Let's say that Lawyer 2 is not interested in buying retiring lawyer's divorce practice. Then the retiring lawyer may sell the personal injury practice to Lawyer 2, and the divorce practice to Lawyer 3, who may be a lawyer specializing in family law. Perhaps the retiring lawyer is not leaving the private practice of law, but she has decided to specialize only in divorce work. She no longer wishes to handle personal injury cases. Retiring lawyer may ethically sell the personal injury practice to Lawyer 2. If the retiring lawyer does this, she must no longer practice personal injury law. Retiring lawyer cannot sell some personal injury cases and keep others.

E. What Notice Must Clients Receive When a Lawyer Sells a Law Practice?

A lawyer or a law firm may sell or purchase a law practice, or an area of law practice, including good will, if the following conditions are satisfied:

1. The seller ceases to engage in the private practice of law, or in the area of practice that has been sold, in the geographic area in which the practice has been conducted;

2. The entire practice, or the entire area of practice, is sold to one or more lawyers or law firms;

3. The seller gives written notice to each of the seller's clients regarding:

   - the proposed sale;

   - the client's right to retain other counsel or to take possession of the file; and

   - the fact that the client's consent to the transfer of the client's files will be presumed if the client does not take any action or does not otherwise object within ninety (90) days of receipt of the notice.

If a client cannot be given notice, the representation of that client may be transferred to the purchaser only upon entry of an authorizing order by a court having jurisdiction. The seller may disclose to the court, in camera, information relating to the representation only to the extent necessary to obtain an order authorizing the transfer of a file. One final requirement: the fees charged clients must not be increased by reason of the sale.

F. What Is the Sale of Goodwill?

Beyond the furniture, the law books, and other physical assets, the major asset being sold in the sale of a law practice is goodwill—the lawyer's reputation and the tendency of clients to continue to call the same telephone number or to go to the same office to obtain future legal services. If a lawyer sells a practice, but then reopens the same type of practice across the street, the buyer is not getting the benefit of buying the goodwill. Even if that behavior is not explicitly contrary to the terms of the sales contract, it is certainly a violation of the spirit of the sale. Under Rule 1.17, a sale of a practice is permissible only if the seller ceases to engage in the private practice of law, or in the area of practice that has been sold. Remember that goodwill is considered to be an asset in a law practice, and the ethical rules have more recently recognized the importance and value of goodwill.

In sum, there are many good reasons to sell a practice, the most prominent being the ability to maximize the value of an asset that has been built up over years or decades. If handled correctly, the sale of a law practice is ethical and can generate a sum of cash that can be used for retirement or other needs.

CHAPTER 10

Conflicts of Interests: Concurrent

One of the most important (and complicated) areas of Professional Responsibility involves conflicts of interest. Regardless of the area of law in which a lawyer practices, conflicts of interest are always an ongoing issue. Every time a lawyer takes on a new client, there is the possibility that an impermissible conflict of interest exists. When you become a lawyer, you must be ever-vigilant to avoid conflicts of interests and the problems those conflicts bring.

The Rules of Professional Responsibility govern conflicts in several different areas: they govern conflicts between current clients, conflicts between current clients and former clients, and conflicts involving corporate clients.

A. What Are the Main Policies Behind the Conflicts of Interest Rules?

All of the conflicts rules provide a balance among policies and client interests. One policy of the conflicts rules is the desire to protect the loyalty between a lawyer and a client. Clients must trust their lawyers. To achieve an adequate level of trust, the lawyer must have an undivided loyalty to the client. Indeed, this loyalty is part of the fiduciary duty the lawyer owes to a client apart from any set of rules. Conflicts rules are designed first and foremost to protect client loyalty.

In addition to the duty of loyalty, there is the lawyer's duty to keep the client's matters confidential. The conflicts rules are designed to protect confidentiality by removing situations in which a lawyer might be tempted to disclose confidential information disadvantageously to the client.

The principals of loyalty and client confidentiality could lead to rules preventing many representations, leaving lawyers overly limited as to whom they can take on as clients. The conflicts of interest rules try to strike a balance by allowing clients, former clients, and others to consent to some conflicts of interest. As a result, even when you've identified a conflict of interest, in most cases, the clients can waive the conflict.

Thus, a conflict of interest does not automatically mean that the representation cannot continue. It may mean only that you need to get both clients to provide a waiver that will allow the matter to proceed. Remember: any consent or waiver can occur only with full disclosure both of the risks accompanying the situation and of the alternatives to the conflicted representation. Consent must be a knowing and informed waiver.

B. What Are the Conflicts Issues Between Current Clients?

The duty of loyalty lies behind all conflicts rules, and in particular, behind the conflict of interest rules related to current clients. A client must believe that his or her lawyer will protect the client's interests and confidences first and foremost and will focus on the client's case above all others. When a lawyer has a conflict of interest, that duty of loyalty is threatened and there is a danger that the lawyer's divided loyalty will harm the client.

The conflict of interest rules guide lawyers in identifying situations in which the potential for harm to a client is real. The main rule is Rule 1.7, which deals with conflicts that have the potential to harm current clients. The first step in any analysis of a conflict of interest problem is to determine whether there is an actual conflict of interest. If the situation presents a conflict, the next question is whether the representation is still permissible with client consent, or whether it is not possible, regardless of client consent.

C. Is There a Conflict of Interest?

Lawyers must scrutinize a potential representation for conflicts before they can take the representation. If a lawyer determines that a particular case presents no conflict, then the lawyer may take the representation but must continually be wary of developing conflicts that were not present at the beginning of the representation. If a conflict of interest develops, the lawyer may be required to withdraw from the representation if no client consent can be obtained.

A conflict of interest regarding a current client exists in two situations. First, a lawyer has a concurrent conflict of interest, under Rule 1.7(a), if the lawyer represents a client and that representation is *directly adverse* to another client. Second, a lawyer has a concurrent conflict of interest, as provided by Rule 1.7(a)(2), if the lawyer's representation of a client may be *materially limited* by the lawyer's own interest, or by the lawyer's responsibilities to another client, a former client, or another person. A small chance of a material limitation does not create a conflict; there must be a significant risk that the representation of the client will be materially limited.

D. What Does It Mean for a Representation to Be "Directly Adverse?"

In the first situation involving a conflict of interest, the lawyer's representation of a client is directly adverse to that of another client. The conflict is between two current clients. Perhaps a lawyer represents the client in an employment dispute with her employer. Perhaps the employer has asked the lawyer to represent it in a debt collection matter against the client. In the debt collection matter, the lawyer would be representing the employer against the client. The lawyer's representation of the employer against the client presents a conflict of interest because the lawyer is adverse to a current client in the debt collection matter. Thus, the lawyer is "directly adverse" to a current client.

Advocating against a current client does damage to the concept of loyalty, which is why it is prohibited by the conflict of interest rules. This prohibition applies even when the matter in which the lawyer is advocating against the client concerns an entirely different subject from the one in which the lawyer represents the client. In our example, the fact that the first dispute is wholly unrelated to the employer debt collection action is irrelevant. If the lawyer represents the employer against the client, the client will feel betrayed. She might no longer trust the lawyer in his role as her lawyer in the employment matter. The lawyer might also learn confidential information in his role as her lawyer in the employment action that he might be tempted to use in the debt collection matter. In addition, the employer might doubt the lawyer's loyalty to it as the result of lawyer's representation of the client.

In a "directly adverse" setting, the representation of one client against another will create a conflict.

E. What Is a "Materially Limited" Representation?

The second situation in which there is a conflict of interest involving a current client is where a significant risk exists that a lawyer's personal interest or a lawyer's responsibilities to another current client, a former client, or any other person will materially limit the lawyer's representation of a client. Along with the "directly adverse" setting, the risk of a "materially limited" representation setting is one in which there is a risk of harm to the client. The conflict exists if there is a significant risk that the lawyer's independent professional judgment will be circumscribed by differing interests of other clients, former clients or other parties, or the lawyer. Recognizing the conflict does not mean that the representation cannot occur; it simply means that the lawyer must analyze the situation and determine if the conflict can be waived.

A very common situation in which conflicts arise is when a lawyer represents two clients (on the same side) in the same litigation matter. Perhaps the lawyer is considering representing both driver and passenger in a vehicle struck by another car. This is often called a dual representation. Both injured parties want the lawyer to represent them in an action against the defendant. The driver suffered minor injuries, but the passenger suffered significant injuries with lasting effects. The lawyer should recognize that at some point, she might come to know confidential information about the driver or passenger that could be useful to the other in the action against defendant or in a possible claim by one client against the other. For example, the lawyer might come to know facts about the driver that would support a claim by the passenger against the driver. In such a situation, the lawyer would have both a duty to disclose the information to the passenger and a duty of confidentiality to the driver—and thus could not disclose the information to the passenger in deciding whether to accept such a representation. Therefore, in determining whether to represent both parties, the lawyer must consider whether there is a significant risk that her representation of the passenger might be "materially limited" by her representation of driver, or vice versa. Since there is a likely material limitation in the representation, a waiver from the clients would likely be required.

F. Can Conflicts of Interest Arise with Former Clients?

The answer is yes. Former clients are another source of conflicts of interest. Such conflicts are governed by Rule 1.9 but the representation may also present a conflict of interest under Rule 1.7. While lawyers do not owe former clients the same duty of loyalty as they do current clients, the duty of confidentiality under Rule 1.6 does not stop simply because the lawyer-client relationship ends.

Consider a lawyer deciding whether to represent a client in an action against her employer. Let's say the lawyer represented the employer in the past with regard to several contractual matters. However, the lawyer no longer represents the employer on such matters. The client would like the lawyer to represent her in a tort matter against the employer. Rule 1.9, the professional responsibility rule relating to former clients, might or might not prevent the lawyer from representing the client against the employer. But the lawyer might have a concurrent conflict of interest under Rule 1.7 because she might have obtained confidential information from the employer in the past that would now be useful to the client. Under Rule 1.7, the lawyer cannot share that information with the client. The lawyer's representation of client thus might be "materially limited" by the duties of confidentiality the lawyer owes to the employer. In addition, the lawyer might think highly of the employer and thus may not be as aggressive in advocating for the client as she would otherwise be. At the time the lawyer is initially considering whether to represent the client, the lawyer must consider such possible scenarios to determine whether there is a significant risk that her representation of the client could be materially limited by her former representation of employer. If there is a significant risk, then the lawyer has a Rule 1.7 conflict of interest.

G. Can a Lawyer's Personal Interest Cause a Conflict of Interest?

The answer is also yes. A lawyer's own personal or business interests can be another source of a conflict of interest. Perhaps a lawyer is considering representing a client on a claim against the city. Perhaps the lawyer feels that she owes her success to the mentoring and guidance she received from the City Attorney when she worked there years before. The lawyer's personal relationship with the City Attorney might interfere with the lawyer's ability to render independent professional judgment on behalf of the client, or the lawyer might not pursue the client's claim as aggressively as she would otherwise do, or the lawyer might limit the possible avenues the client could take. The lawyer must consider such possibilities in determining whether there is a significant risk that her representation of the client might be materially limited by her loyalty to the City Attorney. If there is a significant risk, then the lawyer has a conflict of interest.

Other sources of personal interest conflicts include the lawyer's business involvements and relationships with other lawyers involved in a matter. For example, the fact that the opposing party is represented by the lawyer's mother may create a significant risk of a material limitation of the client's representation.

When a matter involves a question of the propriety of the lawyer's conduct, the lawyer's own interest in defending himself or herself might interfere with the representation. A lawyer who serves on a board of directors of a corporation might not be able to represent the corporation with regard to certain matters because of a significant risk that the representation will be materially limited. For example, the lawyer might not be able to handle a matter involving a board decision because the lawyer was involved in the decision-making process.

Further, a conflict of interest can exist when the source of the limitation on the client's representation is a third person. The situation of a third party paying the legal fees for a client often presents a setting in which there is a conflict of interest. This is often called a third-party payor. Perhaps a lawyer is considering representing a client in a divorce matter. The client's father contacted the lawyer and has explained that he will pay the lawyer for the service rendered to the client. Rule 1.8 states that in such arrangements, the client must give her informed consent, the lawyer must take care to not allow the father to interfere with the lawyer's independence and professional judgment, and the lawyer must protect the client's confidential information as required by Rule 1.6. If the lawyer believes that there is a significant risk that the father will interfere with the lawyer-client relationship, and if lawyer believes that the result of the father's intrusion will be a material limitation on the lawyer's representation of the client, the lawyer has a conflict of interest that needs more attention.

H. If There Is a Conflict of Interest, Can the Attorney Continue with Client Consent?

The answer for almost all conflict of interest issues is likely yes. There are some conflicted representations where a lawyer cannot undertake the case even if the client is willing to give informed consent. If a representation presents a concurrent conflict under Rule 1.7, the lawyer cannot represent the client in the matter if the representation is prohibited by law, if it involves two or more adverse clients in the same litigation, or if the lawyer reasonably believes that he or she cannot render competent representation of the client. If none of these three conditions applies, then lawyer may represent the client if each affected client renders informed consent, confirmed in writing.

The representation cannot continue if it is prohibited by law. Some states have laws prohibiting a lawyer from representing two defendants in a capital murder case, or a husband and wife in a divorce case. The legislatures of those states have decided that the risk of adverse impact on the representations that such conflicted representations might create, and the appeals such representations would generate, justify banning such multiple representations altogether.

In addition, a lawyer in a litigation matter, or in any other matter before a tribunal, cannot represent two clients who are asserting claims against each other. A lawyer cannot represent a client in pursuing a personal injury claim against a corporation and also defend the corporation against the client's claim. There is simply no way that a lawyer can comply with the duties of confidentiality and loyalty that the lawyer owes to both the client and the corporation.

Even if no law prevents a representation in a conflict situation, Rule 1.7(b) states that a lawyer cannot handle a representation if the lawyer does not reasonably believe that the lawyer can provide competent and diligent representation to the client whose representation presents the concurrent conflict of interest. In other words, if a lawyer does not reasonably believe that he or she can provide competent and diligent representation to the client, the lawyer cannot ask the client to give informed consent to the conflict.

I. How Does a Client Provide Informed Consent?

If a representation presents a conflict of interest, but no law prohibits the representation, and the lawyer reasonably believes that she can render competent and diligent representation, the lawyer may ask the client to consent to the conflicted representation. Rule 1.7(b) requires that the consent be informed and confirmed in writing. The requirement of the writing assists clients in understanding the seriousness of the issue of consent to the conflict of interest.

To give informed consent, a client must be aware of all the reasonably foreseeable ways that the conflict could adversely affect the client. Under Rule 1.0, which defines informed consent, the lawyer must explain the material risks and the available alternatives to the representation. Then the client must give consent in writing, which most typically involves the lawyer preparing a written waiver or writing that confirms the client's oral consent. The lawyer sends the writing to the client in a reasonable amount of time after the client gives oral consent. An email can constitute a writing although often lawyers will prepare a separate and/or formal letter.

If the conflict is between two current clients, both clients must give consent for the representation to occur because both have interests are at issue. The lawyer (or lawyers if the clients are represented by different lawyers in the same firm) will sit down with the clients individually and explain the loyalty issues that might arise as well as the confidentiality issues such a situation might present.

In larger law firms, it is very common for one lawyer in a firm to take on a new client that happens to be adverse to another firm client. In that situation, the lawyer for the new client must disclose the fact that the firm already represents the adverse party—likely in unrelated matters. The lawyer must explain to the new client that this presents a conflict of interest because the firm cannot take on a new client where the firm already represents another client on a matter adverse to the new client. It does not matter for conflicts purposes whether the matters are completely unrelated to each other. It could be that the new client wants the lawyer to handle a lease between the client and a tenant who is represented by the firm in another matter. Perhaps the firm represents the tenant in a personal injury matter completely unrelated to the leasing matter. There is still a conflict of interest.

If the firm takes on the new client when it also represents the adverse party in the leasing matter, i.e., the tenant, there is a conflict of interest that must be waived by both parties. In the situation described above, it is likely that the parties will waive the conflict of interest. The new matter is transactional and there likely will not be any disagreements between the parties as they negotiate the lease terms.

What if, however, the new matter actually involves litigation, with the new client wanting to sue the tenant for breach of the lease contract? The tenant who is represented by the firm in the other matter likely will not take too kindly to the fact that the firm wants to represent a new client who is suing the tenant—even if it's a completely unrelated matter. The tenant will probably feel that the firm is being disloyal: how can the firm represent the tenant, and then represent another party who is suing the tenant? In this circumstance, it would be possible for the clients to waive, just as with any other concurrent conflict. However, the clients might decide not to waive. If the clients do not waive the conflict of interest, the attorney cannot take on the new representation.

Note also that even when clients grant consent, a client can revoke that consent at any time. A client has a right to terminate a representation at any time, which includes terminating or revoking consent. Remember, however, that if a client does revoke consent, the revocation does not automatically mean that the lawyer or lawyers must withdraw from representation. If a representation is underway, then it would not be fair to the represented client to simply end the representation—the lawyer would have duties to that client as well. To guard against this situation, a lawyer can put language in a conflict waiver that states that the client cannot revoke consent while also insisting that the representation of the other client must cease. This type of language protects the client with whom the conflict arises from unilaterally losing attorney representation if the other client revokes consent.

J.   Can a Client Consent to Waive Future Conflicts?

Sometimes it is beneficial for a lawyer to have a client waive not only a present or concurrent conflict of interest, but also a conflict that might arise later. Lawyers often call these types of waivers advanced waivers. At the beginning of a new representation, there might be no conflicts and no risk of a material limitation on the representation. But what about a potential future conflict that neither the party nor the lawyer knows about at the start? A lawyer might want to ensure that if a conflict arises, the lawyer will not be forced to withdraw from this, or another, representation. If such a conflict does arise, an advanced waiver of a conflict may be enforceable—if the conflict is not one of the types described above for which consent is not possible.

If a conflict of interest does arise (and this happens frequently in larger law firms), then the waiver may be valid if the waiving party, at the time of agreeing to the waiver, understands the risks involved in the representation and waiver.

As long as clients are well informed about the risks of the advance waiver and are sophisticated, future or advanced waivers are permissible. There are some cases, however, where courts have invalidated advanced waivers—typically, in circumstances where the client who waived was unsophisticated or the waiver did not spell out the specific risks of the waiver.

Remember that an advanced waiver of a future conflict is actual consent to the conflict, so the waiver must be an informed consent. In addition, the waiver must, as with any other informed consent to a conflict of interest, be confirmed in writing. Thus, the waiver itself must be in writing or there must—at a minimum— be written confirmation of the waiver (which can include an email). Often, waivers of future conflicts will be a part of an initial engagement letter or attorney-client agreement, so the client signs the waiver when he or she signs the engagement letter.

K. What if a Conflict Arises During the Course of the Representation?

A situation can occur where a conflict arises during the course of a representation. Perhaps a party is added to a litigation matter and no one contemplated the party being added when the lawsuit was originally filed. What happens if a conflict becomes apparent and the client refuses to consent to the representation due to the conflict? In this situation, the lawyer must withdraw. Rule 1.16(a) makes withdrawal mandatory because the continued representation would violate Rule 1.7.

What if a lawyer properly represented multiple plaintiffs in a single matter (i.e., they waived the conflict, with informed consent confirmed in writing), and some of the plaintiffs now take positions adverse to other plaintiffs? Here, the lawyer probably should withdraw from the entire representation because there would be a material limitation on her ability to represent one plaintiff if another plaintiff, for example, had cross-claims against the first plaintiff, or just disagreed with the trial strategy. Representing multiple clients is very risky because a lawyer cannot control how a case will proceed. It is always a possibility that parties who began a representation aligned will become contentious as a matter proceeds. Before proceeding with any sort of multi-party representation, a lawyer must ensure that the clients have signed a waiver for the conflict of interest.

L. Can a Firm Drop an Existing Client to Take on a New Client?

Law firms sometimes consider terminating a client representation in order to accept an engagement adverse to that client. In some instances, the firm wants to drop a small client to accept a more lucrative matter from a new client. In other instances, the adverse representation is for another, current client of the firm. You might assume that a lawyer may terminate representation of the disfavored client so long as doing so will not have a material adverse effect on that client's interests. But this is not true: the so-called "hot potato" doctrine may frustrate the firm's attempt to disengage.

The majority view, expressed in a frequently-quoted opinion, is that "[a] firm may not drop a client like a hot potato, especially if it is in order to keep happy a far more lucrative client." *Picker Int'l, Inc. v. Varian Assocs., Inc.*, 670 F. Supp. 1363, 1365 (N.D. Ohio 1987), *aff'd*, 869 F.2d 578 (Fed. Cir. 1989).

If a representation has been properly terminated before a conflict arises, a firm is generally permitted to be adverse to the former client on matters unrelated to the prior representation. However, dropping a current client to take on a new matter adverse to the dropped client may be a risky proposition. If this action is to be pursued at all, it is prudent to have some time delay between terminating the representation of one client and engaging the new client who may have a matter adverse to the former client.

CHAPTER 11

Conflicts of Interests: Corporations

When an attorney represents a corporation or entity, does the attorney also represent others in the corporation? For example, does the attorney represent shareholders? Sister and subsidiary corporations? Officers? Limited partners? These are common questions for lawyers who represent corporations. The ethical rule that addresses issues involving a corporate and/or in-house corporate counsel is Rule 1.13, Organization as Client. Rule 1.13(a) provides that a lawyer employed or retained by an organization represents the organization acting through its duly authorized constituents. This is an important statement: the corporation, not individuals, is the client.

The types of conflicts that exist in corporate practice mirror those that exist in conflicts generally, and the resolution of those conflicts turn on the same general themes: loyalty, preservation of confidential information, and the exercise of independent professional judgment by the attorney.

A.   Who Is the Client for Conflict Purposes?

A corporate attorney, whether an in-house lawyer or a law firm that serves as counsel to the company, owes a duty to act in accordance with the interests of the corporate entity itself. The client is the corporation. In a conflict context, this means that a lawyer employed to represent an organization represents the interests of the organization as defined by its responsible agents acting pursuant to the organization's decision-making procedures. Thus, the attorney's duty to preserve confidential information and to exercise independent professional judgment run to the entity, and not to other constituents within the organization.

This unique relationship between corporate attorney and corporation as client means that conflict and confidentiality issues will often arise when the attorney, although representing the corporation, is dealing with constituents or members whose interests may diverge from those of the corporation. For example, the corporation's attorney could be talking to an employee who discloses that he or she has been using drugs while on the job. The lawyer needs to obtain this type of information to protect the corporation, but the information has the potential to be used adversely against the employee.

The challenge for the corporate attorney is to deal with these constituents or employees fairly while at the same time advancing the corporation's interests in obtaining necessary information and protecting its institutional interests. This is not always easy. One of the most important things for corporate attorneys to do, however, is to begin any conversation with an employee or other constituent with the reminder that they are the corporation's attorney and not the employee or constituent's attorney.

Pursuant to Rule 1.13(d) and Rule 4.3, the corporate lawyer must make clear to those with whom he or she is dealing that the corporation is the client and that information provided by those individuals is privileged outside the corporation but not as to the corporation itself. The lawyer's role as counsel for the entity should be clarified in any situation where the interest of the constituent has the potential of being adverse to the interest of the corporation.

A corporate lawyer may, subject to the agreement of the corporation, concurrently represent the corporation and one or more of its existing or former constituents. In order to do so, the attorney must insure that the general conflict of interest provisions of Rule 1.7 are scrupulously followed. This requires first that the attorney reasonably believe that he or she can adequately represent both the corporation and the constituents. In determining whether such representation is possible, the attorney must analyze what effect the dual representation will have on the attorney's ability to exercise independent professional judgment on behalf of the corporation. In addition, the attorney must obtain the consent of the organization. In order to obtain such consent, the attorney must clearly explain the impact of the dual representation, and the consent must be obtained from an appropriate official other than the person who is to be jointly represented.

B. Does a Corporate Lawyer Have Special Duties of Confidentiality to the Corporation?

The answer is yes. The in-house lawyer has a duty to protect the client's confidences—to not divulge information relating to the representation—unless the client gives informed consent or the disclosure is impliedly authorized to carry out the representation. For in-house counsel, "representation" is not a single project or issue; it involves numerous separate and distinct projects and issues. The in-house lawyer must continually use professional judgment and discretion to determine which employees are appropriate recipients of any information relating to the representation.

C. How Does the Corporate Lawyer Protect the Organization by Reporting Out?

Rule 1.13(b) has been recently revised to permit the corporate lawyer to "report up" to protect the corporation. The obligation to "report up" is one of several gatekeeper functions imposed on in-house or corporate counsel. The "reporting up" obligation under Rule 1.13(b) applies when a lawyer for an organization knows that an officer, employee, or other person associated with the organization is engaged in action that is a violation of a legal obligation to the organization that is likely to result in substantial injury to the organization. In such a situation, the lawyer must proceed as is reasonably necessary in the best interest of the organization. The lawyer must refer the matter to a higher authority in the organization, up to the highest authority that can act on behalf of the organization as determined by applicable law.

This revision is a fairly new aspect of the rules. As a result of the various economic crises in the past decade, it was determined that a lawyer should be able to report wrongdoing when it will affect the corporation—the true client of the lawyer. So if a lawyer learns that someone within the corporation has acted or refused to act in a way that violates a legal obligation to the organization, or that constitutes a crime, fraud, or other violation of law that could be imputed to, and is likely to result in substantial injury to, the organization, the lawyer has a duty to report that knowledge to the leaders at the corporation. A lawyer must always act in the best interest of the organization, which in many cases requires bringing the wrongful conduct to the attention of higher authority.

If the organization's highest authority neglects to address a crime or fraud in a timely and appropriate way, the lawyer may even reveal confidential information relating to the representation to prevent substantial injury to the organization. Rule 1.13 helps to sharpen the lawyer's focus on the best interests of the organization.

CHAPTER 12

Conflicts of Interests: Former Clients and Imputation

A lawyer who no longer represents a client still owes that client a duty of confidentiality and loyalty. Certainly, these duties may be less than those owed to a current client, but these duties still exist. Rule 1.9 prohibits representations in which confidential information might be in danger of use or disclosure, as well as situations in which the lawyer appears to have switched sides in a matter. Rule 1.9 states that a lawyer may not represent a client in the following scenario: when the interests of a client are (1) *materially adverse* to the interests of a former client of the lawyer; and (2) the representation is in the *same or a substantially related matter*, unless the former client gives informed consent for the representation.

The policy behind this rule is that if the representation is in the same or a substantially related matter and if the client is materially adverse to the former client, the lawyer would confront conflicting duties: to disclose the information to the current client and to keep the information confidential on behalf of the former client. Rule 1.9 is crafted to prevent this conflict from occurring by focusing the on the particular confidential information in question. Rule 1.9 thus prevents a lawyer from, in effect, switching sides in a matter. At the same time, the rule accomplishes the goals of not unduly constraining lawyers in the private practice of law.

A. What Is a "Same or a Substantially Related Matter?"

Matters are substantially related if they involve the same transaction or legal dispute, or if there is otherwise a substantial risk that confidential factual information that would normally have been obtained in the prior representation would materially advance the client's position in the later matter. For example, if a lawyer recently represented a client and learned intimate details about the client's financial situation, Rule 1.9 would prohibit the lawyer from the later representation of a second client, the first client's husband, in the parties' divorce, even if the lawyer is no longer representing the first client (the wife).

Consider the language from the Restatement (Third) of the Law of Governing Lawyers section 132 (2000), which states in part:

> The current matter is substantially related to the earlier matter if: (1) the current matter involves the work the lawyer performed for the former client; or (2) there is a substantial risk that representation of the present client will involve the use of information acquired in the course of representing the former client, unless that information has become generally known.

The principal concern with former client conflicts of interest is the use of confidential information learned through a former representation that can help a new client but would hurt the former client.

B. Who Is a Former Client?

This question is actually surprisingly difficult to answer. If a party is a current client, Rule 1.7 applies for concurrent conflicts of interest. If a client is a former client, then Rule 1.9 applies. The key is that a lawyer-client relationship exists if a party reasonably believes that a lawyer represents that party. If the lawyer has represented a client in the past, that client is a current client if the client reasonably believes that the lawyer still represents the client. The lawyer's belief is not relevant.

If a lawyer sends a client a letter stating that the representation has concluded, then the party could not have a reasonable belief that the lawyer-client relationship continues to exist. Such a letter is called a "disengagement letter" and these types of letters do clarify that the client is a former client. However, lawyers often do not want to terminate an attorney-client relationship when a particular matter ends because they hope their clients will return with future business. As a result, there is often no certainty with regard to the status of a party as a current or former client.

C. Can Client Consent Waive the Conflict?

Yes. If a representation presents a conflict of interest under Rule 1.9, a lawyer may not handle the representation unless the former client gives informed consent, confirmed in writing. Informed consent requires the lawyer to explain to the former client the material risks and the reasonably available alternatives to the conflicted representation. The requirement that the consent be confirmed in writing means that the former client must give consent in writing or the lawyer must prepare a waiver or email confirming the former client's oral consent and must send it to the former client within a reasonable amount of time. A former client usually has little to lose by refusing consent. The new representation may have little effect on the former client. But former clients can still say 'no' and choose not to provide consent. In that circumstance, the lawyer will need to decline the representation of the new client—plain and simple. This is a difficult situation, but the former client's decision controls.

D. Does the Taint of One Conflict Spill Over to Another Lawyer in the Same Law Firm?

Perhaps surprisingly, the answer is yes, and we call this concept the "imputation" of the conflict. Rule 1.10 addresses the imputation of a former client conflict. The rule states that if a lawyer has a conflict of interest, all lawyers in the same firm have the same conflict. The imputation results from the belief that a firm of lawyers is essentially one lawyer. If a lawyer cannot represent a new client because of Rule 1.9 (i.e., the new client was adverse to a former client), then no lawyer in the firm can represent that client either. The lawyer's conflict of interest is imputed to the entire law firm.

There is one situation, however, where imputation does not occur. Imputation does not occur if the basis of the disqualification is a personal interest of the lawyer versus an actual conflict of interest under Rule 1.7 or Rule 1.9, as long as the situation does not present a significant risk of materially limiting the representation. In other words, an imputed disqualification can be waived in these circumstances when it is simply a lawyer's personal interest. For example, if a lawyer is conflicted out of a representation because, for example, the lawyer's wife is a lawyer involved on the opposite side of transaction, this conflict may not be imputed to other members of the lawyer's firm.

E. What Duties Does the Lawyer Have to the Former Client?

Even though a lawyer's representation of a former client has ended, a lawyer still has a duty of confidentiality to that client. Rule 1.6 establishes the duty of confidentiality generally. A lawyer cannot disclose information relating to a client's representation and this duty continues after the conclusion of the representation. The attorney-client privilege also applies after the conclusion of the representation. Rule 1.9 has its own confidentiality clause with regard to former clients. Rule 1.9(c) clarifies that a lawyer may not use information relating to a former client's representation to that former client's disadvantage unless the rules so permit, or the information has become generally known.

F. What Happens When a Lawyer Transitions from One Law Firm to Another?

If an attorney transitions from one law firm to another, it is quite possible she will bring all her conflicts of interest with her and that these conflicts of interest will be imputed to others at the new firm as well. Let's say a lawyer starts a new job at a firm and wants to bring over a new client as well. However, let's also assume that the law firm wants to take on a client that will actually be adverse to the new client in an unrelated matter. What conflicts will the lawyer bring with her to the new firm?

A helpful way to think about this issue is to begin by asking whether the lawyer would be disqualified from representing her client's adversary if the lawyer had *not* changed firms—that is, would the lawyer have a conflict of interest with another client if she were still at her old firm? These situations arise both as to conflicts between current clients under Rule 1.7 and conflicts with former clients under Rule 1.9. If the lawyer would not have had a conflict at her former firm, then she will not have a conflict at her new firm and the new firm would not be disqualified from any representation/s. However, if the lawyer would have had a conflict of interest had she stayed at her old firm (and took on the new client), then the lawyer does not shed the conflict when she changes firms.

If the new hire does have a conflict, the second question is whether the new firm is also disqualified from taking on any representation/s adverse to the client. The starting point for a discussion of these issues is Rule 1.10, the imputed disqualification rule. Rule 1.10(a) sets out the traditional per se rule that forms the basic standard: while lawyers are associated in a firm, none of them shall knowingly represent a client when any one of them practicing alone would be prohibited from doing so by the rules on conflicts of interest with current and former clients (Rules 1.7 and 1.9).

Rule 1.10 is premised on the undivided loyalty owed to a client, as well as the presumption that lawyers associated in a firm share or have access to confidential information concerning each other's clients. For example, an attorney cannot represent a client in a personal injury case while his partner is suing the same client for specific performance on an entirely unrelated option agreement.

Under Rule 1.7, the discussion as to current clients essentially ends there. Consider this example. If the former firm of the new hire is representing an adversary of the new firm in the same or a substantially related pending matter, and the transplanted lawyer has any material confidential information, the new firm is disqualified from taking on the new client. In essence, since the lawyer changing firms would himself be disqualified under either

Rule 1.7 or Rule 1.9, his new firm is also disqualified. In other words, the conflict of the lawyer is imputed to the new firm.

Many states, however, provide for a narrow exception permitting the representation in limited circumstances even when the new hire is disqualified as a result of a conflict. Rule 1.10 explains a concept known as "screening," which separates the new lawyer from any data or information, and denies the lawyer the ability to gain or provide information about the matter. Screens are also referred to as ethical walls. Such screens or ethical walls are typically created by computer software that locks down any attorney's access to prohibited information. If a lawyer is screened from a matter, then it's possible the conflict will not be imputed.

Note, however, that nothing can be done to prevent disqualification of the new firm if the newly associated attorney had substantial material information or involvement in the pending matter at his or her old firm. Under these circumstances, screening is not an adequate protection and the new firm will have to withdraw.

On the other hand, what if the new hire has no material protected information about the case from the old firm? In an ongoing case, the new hire is still personally disqualified from representing the opposing party at the new firm in that same or a substantially related matter, but the conflict is not imputed to the firm.

In sum, when can screening apply? Screening applies when a new hire may have had some information or involvement about a case at the old firm, but the involvement was not substantial. In such a situation, the new lawyer would still be personally disqualified. However, in this situation and only in this situation, Rule 1.10(d) provides that the new firm is not disqualified if the new hire is promptly screened from participation in the matter—and receives no part of the fee paid to the new firm.

G. What Constitutes Adequate Screening?

Rule 1.10(e) then sets out in detail the requirements for adequate screening: (1) material information in the possession of the personally disqualified attorney must be isolated from the firm; (2) the personally disqualified attorney must be isolated from contact with the client and with witnesses for or against the client; (3) the personally disqualified attorney and the firm cannot discuss the matter with each other; (4) notice and an affidavit from the personally disqualified attorney containing certain prescribed information must be sent to the former client; and (5) the personally disqualified attorney and the new firm must reasonably believe that the screening will be effective in preventing disclosure of material information to the new firm or its client.

When deciding whether screening is permissible, it is critical to look carefully at Rule 1.10(e). For example, suppose a two-lawyer firm that represents a wife in a pending divorce is hiring a third attorney whose former firm is representing the husband. The new associate had some tangential involvement in the matter at his old firm. In theory, since the new attorney's involvement in the divorce case at the old firm was minimal, it would seem that the new hire could be screened and the new firm would not be disqualified. In practice, it may be impossible in such a small firm to set up an effective screen. Unless the husband and wife both consent to the new firm's continued representation, the new firm may have to withdraw.

There is an additional concern that applies regardless of how large or small the firm is: the possibility that there are other potential conflicts that neither the new hire nor the new firm remembers or knows about. The question then is what type of conflict-checking is permitted in advance of a move to prevent surprise disqualifications from major ongoing cases.

The ethics rules contemplate this possibility through an exception to the duty of confidentiality in Rule 1.6. The subsection states that lawyers changing jobs may reveal to prospective firms or employers, without the consent of the affected clients or ex-clients, "conflict-checking information" including the identity of the lawyer's previous clients and the general subject matter of the representation if not embarrassing or detrimental to the client and limited to the information reasonably necessary to check for conflicts.

Finally, what about the new hire's former firm? Can the old firm represent a new client in bringing an action against an ex-client who had been represented by the lawyer who left the firm? The analysis is very similar to the situation with the new firm when the potential conflict involves former clients. The old firm is not necessarily disqualified from representing a client with interests adverse to those of an ex-client who had been represented by the former partner or associate. However, the firm is not permitted to undertake the representation if the new matter is the same or substantially related to the former representation and if any attorney remaining in the firm has material confidential information.

The rules on imputed disqualification are an attempt to balance a client's right to loyalty and confidentiality against a lawyer's need to be able to change jobs without violating ethical requirements. A careful reading and application of these rules will protect the interests of all concerned.

CHAPTER 13

The Attorney-Client Relationship and the Duty of Confidentiality

Nowadays it is very typical for a client to hire a lawyer for specific legal needs. For example, a client may hire a lawyer to do a client's will for a specific fee. Or perhaps a client will hire a lawyer to represent the client through the course of a trial, but not in any potential appeal. A client and lawyer can limit the scope of a representation in other ways as well. A client might, for example, want the lawyer to pursue only certain avenues of legal argument. This chapter will explore the attorney-client relationship in greater detail.

How do clients and their lawyers divide their responsibilities in a relationship? Can a lawyer limit what the lawyer will choose to do for the client? The answer is yes. Rule 1.2 provides that a lawyer may limit the scope of a representation if the limitation is reasonable and the client gives informed consent. Often the client dictates representation limitations and so the requirement of informed client consent is not a problem. But if the lawyer is the source, the lawyer must fully explain the burdens and risks of such a path and must document the informed consent.

A. Who Makes Decisions During the Course of Representation?

Both the lawyer and client have duties and obligations during the course of a representation. A basic concept is that a client is in charge of the ultimate goals of the representation. Rule 1.2(a) begins by stating that a lawyer shall abide by the client's decisions concerning the objectives of representation. The rule then specifies that the client must decide the following important matters concerning the representation: in a civil matter, whether to settle; in a criminal matter, the plea, whether to waive a jury trial, and whether to testify.

With regard to each of these specific issues, a lawyer should communicate with the client as required by Rule 1.4 and counsel the client about the possible courses of action. While the rule clearly states that the client is the decider of these issues, the client may give the lawyer the authority to decide such matters. Rule 1.2 acknowledges that the client may give the lawyer authority to take specific action on the client's behalf. Of course, the client may revoke this authority just as any other principal may revoke authority earlier granted.

Traditionally, just as the goals or objectives of the representation were seen as the choice of the client, the means of achieving the objects were seen as the lawyer's decision. Rule 1.2(a) does not, however, explicitly grant that power to the lawyer. The rule states that the lawyer must consult with the client as to the means to be used. Decisions relating to technical, legal, and tactical matters are usually left to the lawyer.

Establishing a lawyer-client relationship for purposes of a matter does impliedly authorize the lawyer to take certain actions on behalf of the client. The nature of the authorization depends on the nature of the representation.

B. What if the Client Engages in Fraudulent or Criminal Activity?

The Rules clearly state that a lawyer may not assist a client in criminal or fraudulent conduct. Likewise, a lawyer may not counsel a client to commit a crime or fraud or engage in conduct that is criminal or fraudulent. However, Rule 1.2(d) clarifies that a lawyer may explain the consequences of possible course of action to the client. A lawyer may also assist a client in determining whether particular conduct is criminal or fraudulent and in determining the validity, scope, and meaning of any possibly applicable laws.

However, a lawyer does not endorse or accept a client's views or actions simply because the lawyer represents the client. Even people with distasteful beliefs or people who have committed distasteful acts should have legal representation.

C. What Is the Duty of Confidentiality?

Lawyers have a duty to maintain the confidences of their clients during and after representation. The duty of confidentiality is quite broad and states that a lawyer has a duty not to disclose information relating to the representation of a client. The duty applies to information received from the client in any form as well as to information that comes to the lawyer from any other source. Rule 1.6 states the general duty of confidentiality. This section is reinforced by Rule 1.9(c), which restates the lawyer's duty not to reveal information after the representation has concluded (former clients) and by Rule 1.18(b), which clarifies that the lawyer has a duty not to reveal information even when a prospective client does not become a client. In addition to the duty not to disclose information relation to the representation of a client, there is also a duty not to use the information to the disadvantage of the client.

The rationale for protecting the information is that clients must be free to tell everything to their lawyers so that they may obtain the best and most appropriate legal advice and representation for the situation. A client needs to trust that his attorney will not disclose what the lawyer knows about the client's representation during the representation and even long after the representation ends.

D. How Is the Duty of Confidentiality Different from the Attorney-Client Privilege?

The concepts of lawyer confidentiality and the attorney-client privilege are similar because they both concern information that the lawyer must keep private, and both concepts are protective of the client's ability to confide freely in his or her lawyer. But these two concepts are not the same, and there are critical differences between them that it is important to understand.

The duty of confidentiality is set out in Rule 1.6. This duty has broad application. A lawyer who represents a client in a divorce matter, and who discovers information about the client's relationship with the client's wife while talking to the client's neighbor, has a duty to keep that information confidential. This general confidentiality principle continues after the representation ends and applies to information received about prospective clients as well.

The duty of confidentiality not only forbids *revealing* information, but also proscribes a lawyer's *use* of confidential information about a client to the disadvantage of that client. With regard to former or prospective clients, a lawyer may not use confidential information to the disadvantage of a former or prospective client unless that information has become "generally known."

On the other hand, the attorney-client privilege is a concept from the law of evidence and is found in the common law or statutes of the fifty states. The client, acting through the lawyer, may claim the privilege.

The attorney-client privilege only protects the communications actually had by the client and lawyer, and only extends to information given for the purpose of obtaining legal representation. Any underlying information is not protected if it is available from another source. Therefore, any underlying information will not be covered by the attorney-client privilege simply because the client told it to the lawyer.

By contrast, the ethical duty of client-lawyer confidentiality is quite extensive in terms of what information is protected. It applies not only to matters communicated in confidence by the client but also to all information relating to the representation, regardless of whether it came from the client herself, or from some other source, though a lawyer may be required to testify regarding client communications under compulsion of law. So, if a court determines that particular information is not covered by the attorney-client privilege, it still may be covered by the lawyer's ethical duty of confidentiality. However, under the exception to confidentiality related to compliance with a court order, the lawyer may be compelled to reveal the information nonetheless. Material protected by the lawyer work-product doctrine may also be protected by the duty of confidentiality.

Confidential information is supposed to remain confidential throughout the representation and thereafter, even after the death of the client. Along with the basic principle of maintaining the privacy of client information, a key ethical purpose for maintaining confidentiality is that the information not be used to the detriment of the client, but rather only to advance the client's interests. Even information gained about the client after the representation has concluded is to be kept confidential. However, once information has become generally known, it loses the protection of lawyer confidentiality.

E. How Broadly Is the Duty of Confidentiality Defined?

Remember that the duty of confidentiality is broadly defined. A lawyer has a duty to protect a client's confidential information and this duty relates to all the information relating to the representation of the client—whatever its source. The rule does differentiate between confidential and non-confidential information; all information that relates to the representation of a client is required to kept confidential.

F. What Are the Exceptions to the Duty of Confidentiality?

Although the duty of confidentiality is broad, it is constrained by numerous exceptions, both required and permissive. The real key to understanding the duty of confidentiality is to understand the numerous required and permissive exceptions.

G. When Must a Lawyer Disclose Confidential Information Despite the Duty of Confidentiality?

There are several situations where the lawyer's duty to the tribunal actually trumps the lawyer's duty of confidentiality to the client. These exceptions to the duty of confidentiality are found in Rule 3.3, Candor Toward the Tribunal. A lawyer will need to disclose confidential information to the tribunal in the following four circumstances:

1. To correct a knowingly false statement of material fact or law the lawyer made to a tribunal. Rule 3.3(a)(1).

2. If there is legal authority in the controlling jurisdiction known by the lawyer to be directly adverse to the client's position and that has not been disclosed by opposing counsel. Rule 3.3(a)(2).

3. If a lawyer comes to know that the lawyer, the lawyer's client, or a witness called by the lawyer has offered false material evidence and the lawyer cannot otherwise take reasonable remedial measures. Rule 3.3(a)(3).

4. If a lawyer knows that any person has engaged, is engaging, or is going to engage in criminal or fraudulent conduct relating to a proceeding before a tribunal in which the lawyer represents a client and the lawyer cannot otherwise take reasonable remedial measures. Rule 3.3(b).

H. When *May* a Lawyer Reveal Confidential Information?

Under Rule 1.6, there is a list of exceptions where a lawyer may reveal confidential information. A lawyer *may* reveal confidential information:

1. With the client's informed consent, under Rule 1.6(a);

2. If disclosure is impliedly authorized to carry out the representation, under Rule 1.6(a);

    Example: The most obvious implied authorization is revealing confidential information to persons working with the attorney in the law firm to the extent reasonably necessary.

3. To prevent reasonably likely death or substantial bodily harm, under Rule 1.6(c)(1);

4. To prevent, mitigate, or rectify substantial economic injury to another that is reasonably certain to result or has resulted from a client's commission of a crime or fraud in which the client has used or is using the lawyer's services, under Rule 1.6(c)(2);

5. To secure legal advice about compliance with these Rules, under Rule 1.6(c)(3);

6. To establish or defend a claim in a dispute with a client (including a fee dispute), to defend a criminal charge, disciplinary complaint, or civil claim based on conduct in which a client was involved, or to respond to allegations made in any proceeding regarding the lawyer's representation of a client, under Rule 1.6(c)(4); or

THE ATTORNEY-CLIENT RELATIONSHIP AND THE DUTY OF CONFIDENTIALITY

7. To comply with a court order or other law requiring disclosure, under Rule 1.6(c)(5).

These seven (7) exceptions are the most tested issues on the MPRE related to the duty of confidentiality.

I. If Allowed, How Much Confidential Information Can Be Disclosed by the Attorney?

The required or permitted disclosure of confidential information is not open-ended. The rules state that a lawyer may reveal confidential information only to the extent the lawyer reasonably believes necessary to prevent whatever harm the exception is designed to avoid. This is crucial to remember when making required disclosures that are likely to adversely affect a client. If a lawyer has decided that disclosure is necessary, the client may benefit from self-disclosure and generally should be afforded that opportunity.

J. Can You Tell Your Client That "Everything You Tell Me as Your Attorney Is Confidential?"

The answer here is no—you cannot tell your clients that *everything* they tell you is confidential because it is not. Confidentiality is subject to numerous exceptions, some of which permit a lawyer to disclose confidential information and some of which may require a lawyer to do so. Some lawyers say little or nothing initially to clients about confidentiality, with the result that clients may have incorrect expectations about the extent to which what they tell a lawyer is confidential. That expectation may have formed from an earlier encounter with a lawyer or from watching television. Some lawyers who do talk to their clients about confidentiality tell them that everything that is said will be held in confidence. But that is not accurate. Remember that lawyers have the duty to explain legal representation to a client to the extent reasonably necessary to permit the client to make informed decisions regarding the representation.

K. Can There Be Confidentiality Concerns Among Joint or Co-Clients?

Yes, there are significant confidentiality concerns when representing joint clients. Lawyers may represent two or more clients in the same matter if there is either no conflict of interest among them or the parties have appropriately waived any conflict. However, sharing information among co-clients is very normal and clients do not always understand the ramifications of having one lawyer represents two clients in the same matter. It is assumed that clients accept that their communications with their common lawyer will be shared with their co-client, but kept in confidence as to all others. However, issues arise when the interests of the clients diverge and the lawyer must either withdraw completely or represent only one client (under the waiver terms and conditions). Each client now knows the secrets and confidences of the other.

L. How Long Does the Duty of Confidentiality Last?

The duty of confidentiality begins when a person first seeks representation or advice from a lawyer, even when the lawyer has not yet agreed to represent, or even determined whether to represent, the client. See Rule 1.18, Prospective Client. The duty of confidentiality continues after the lawyer-client relationship ends and does not extinguish with any passage of time, the client's death, or in the case of an organization client, its dissolution. In this way, the duty of confidentiality lasts longer than almost any other duty the lawyer has to a client. Watch for questions that test this concept and suggest that the duty ends after the representation. The duty of confidentiality does not end just because the representation of the client ends.

M. Can a Lawyer Talk to Family and Friends About Their Clients?

The duty of confidentiality forbids any disclosure of confidential information that does not fall within one of the enumerated exceptions. However, this duty does not necessarily recognize the reality that lawyers live outside the office, and it does not recognize that human nature plays a part in confidentiality concerns as well. The safest practice, of course, is for lawyers to never discuss anything relating to their clients with even their most intimate life partners. But, over a lifetime, such a closed and compartmentalized life can exact a toll on psyches and relationships. The best course of action is to govern these discussions by a scrupulous assurance to an anonymity standard: some discussions regarding client matters may happen with family and friends, but a lawyer should make them only with generality and anonymity sufficient to assure that clients or the particular circumstances of their matters are protected from possible identification.

The duty of confidentiality is one of the most important topics to know well for the MPRE. The key is to understand the exceptions, both when a lawyer must reveal confidences and those more common situations where a lawyer may disclose confidential matters.

CHAPTER 14

Zealous Representation and Candor Towards the Tribunal

Various duties make up the idea that a lawyer must provide zealous representation of clients. Among these are the duties that a lawyer must expedite litigation, speak with clients and the court honestly, and advocate fairly for the client.

Rule 1.3 requires reasonable diligence and promptness in representing a client. The client entrusts a legal matter to a lawyer. The lawyer is a fiduciary with regard to the legal matter and thus must act reasonably to advance the client's interest, even to the disadvantage of the lawyer. A lawyer must actively pursue the client's goals within the bounds of the lawyer's good judgement and respect for the rights of the parties and of the court.

As explained by the comments to Rule 1.3, the duty of diligence also requires the lawyer to provide zealous representation to the client. What does it mean to *zealously* represent the client?

A. What Is Zealous Representation?

Lawyers have a strict ethical responsibility to advocate zealously on behalf of their client. Zealous representation does not mean a lawyer should strive to "win" at all costs, if that means harming third parties and adversaries unnecessarily in the process. It means doing everything reasonable to help a client achieve the goals set forth at the outset of the representation.

Here's an example. A client is embroiled in a contentious divorce. He orders his lawyer to exploit every possible weakness in his wife's case in order to prevail—at all costs. One tactic the client's lawyer uses is a constant, unrelenting barrage of motion filings. The case drags on for years. In the end, the client is miserable because he's essentially ruined the family life of his daughter in order to gain the upper hand in the court's distribution of family assets.

Has the attorney conducted himself ethically? It depends. If his motion filings were done solely for the purpose of harassment, then no, the attorney's conduct was not ethical. Even if no ethical violation could be established, however, the attorney probably should have counseled the client about the consequences of such zealous advocacy. Surely the health and happiness of the client's daughter is more important than any material acquisition.

Therefore a balance must be struck in strategizing how to represent a client zealously—between what is achievable within the bounds of the law, and what is reasonable in light of the impact on the parties involved. Certainly, domestic relations cases require peculiar sensibilities that probably would not be relevant in a corporate securities matter. In domestic relations cases, a lawyer has to be careful that her efforts to defeat the adversary do not negatively impact on the lives of children or other family members.

Whatever the issue at bar, overzealous representation presents dangers common to all aspects of the law: a lawyer who does not strike a balance between what is achievable and what could be harmful to others will unnecessarily earn enemies along with the fee.

B. How Does a Lawyer Show Respect for the Rights of Others?

An attorney must show respect for the rights of non-clients. In the context of representing a client, a lawyer may need to deal with all sorts of people. For example, a litigator may talk with witnesses and others as the lawyer investigates and prepares the case. If a lawyer, during the course of representing a client, has contact with a person who is not a client and that person is not represented by a lawyer for the purpose of the matter, the lawyer must abide by several basic standards. Rule 4.3 provides these restrictions.

First, the lawyer may not indicate expressly or by implication that the lawyer is disinterested. If a lawyer represents a client with regard to her personal injury claim against a corporation, for example, the lawyer may want to talk with a witness to see what she knows about the injury to the client. The lawyer cannot lead the witness to believe that she represents the corporation or that she is not representing anyone in the matter.

In fact, the lawyer has an affirmative duty to exercise reasonable efforts to correct any misimpression about a lawyer's role that the witness might have if the lawyer knows or reasonably should know about the witness's confusion. The lawyer should identify her client and explain how the client's interests and the witness's interest may diverge if such an explanation is appropriate for the situation.

A lawyer dealing with an unrepresented person always must be very careful not to create a lawyer-client relationship when the lawyer does not desire to be in one. Courts hold that a lawyer-client relationship exists when the prospective client reasonably believes that such a relationship exists, and if such a relationship exists, then various duties are owed. The lawyer must always be mindful not to make statements or act in ways that could lead a reasonable person to believe that there is a relationship when the lawyer does not intend to have one.

In addition, a lawyer must not give legal advice to otherwise unrepresented people if the lawyer knows or reasonably should know that the interests of the unrepresented person have a reasonable possibility of being in conflict with the client's interest. If the client was injured at a store when she slipped and fell, it is possible that the witness's interests may conflict with the client's interests. The lawyer may advise the witness to get her own lawyer.

Regardless of whether the person with whom the lawyer deals is represented, the lawyer must treat such a person with civility. Rule 4.4 states that a lawyer may not use means that have no purpose other than to embarrass, delay, or burden another person. Also, a lawyer may not obtain evidence in a manner that violates the rights of another person.

C. What Does a Lawyer Do When She Inadvertently Receives Confidential Information?

A lawyer has a duty to preserve the confidentiality of communications and to protect the privileged status of communications. In the modern-day world of emails, texts, and other rapid communications, mistakes may be particularly likely to occur. Sometimes documents are produced, for example, that should not have been produced because they are protected by the attorney-client privilege. Or perhaps a lawyer or a member of the lawyer's office sends an email or fax that contains confidential information and the email or fax is sent mistakenly to the opposing side.

If a lawyer receives a communication relating to the representation of a client and the lawyer knows that the communication was mistakenly sent to the lawyer, under Rule 4.4 (b) the lawyer must promptly notify the sender. This notice allows the sender to be aware of the need to take action to protect any privilege. If a lawyer receives a letter from the opposition's lawyer that begins with "Dear Client," the lawyer reasonably should know that the letter was misdirected. The lawyer must notify the opposition lawyer that she has the letter.

A comment to Rule 1.6 states that a lawyer must act competently to protect against inadvertent or unauthorized disclosure of confidential information. Under Rule 1.1, the duty of competence is judged by a rule of reason. A lawyer should have procedures in place to limit the possibilities of inadvertent disclosure. When an inadvertent disclosure occurs, it is possible that the disclosing lawyer is has not acted competently to protect privileged communications of the client. But it is also possible for a disclosure to occur even when there is competent representation.

D. Does an Attorney Have a Duty of Honesty Toward Third Parties?

Yes, an attorney has a general duty of honesty, as discussed in one of the first chapters of this book. Rule 4.1 is one of the many rules emphasizing the importance of honesty to the practice of law. Other rules dealing with honesty include Rule 3.3, which deals with the duty of candor when a lawyer deals with the tribunal, and Rule 8.4(c), which deals with the general requirement of lawyer honesty. Rule 4.1 specifically deals with a lawyer's duty of honesty when the lawyer deals with third parties such as the opposition and the opposition's lawyer. This duty applies whenever a lawyer is acting in a representative capacity.

E. Does an Attorney Violate the Duty of Honesty by Omitting Information?

Yes. Occasionally a situation arises in which a lawyer faces discipline not for a statement but for a *failure* to make a statement—usually the lawyer's failure to correct a misimpression. For example, assume a lawyer represents a client in a personal injury case arising from a car crash. The lawyer files a negligence action against the driver. The driver is represented by another attorney. Unfortunately, the client dies during the pretrial phase. The lawyer continues to discuss settlement with the opposing attorney but does not tell the opposing attorney that the client has died. In these circumstances, some courts have determined that the lawyer has violated Rule 4.1. The lawyer's failure to disclose the death while pursuing the matter as if the client were alive is an implied misrepresentation. A lawyer in this situation must disclose the client's death to the opposing side and the court in the next contact with those entities after the client's death. If the lawyer did not disclose the information, it's highly likely any settlement that might be reached would be set aside.

F. Does the Duty of Honesty Apply in Settlement Negotiations?

A topic of frequent discussion is whether a lawyer, during the course of a negotiation, may take any liberties with the truth as a posturing technique. In the context of a settlement negotiation, for example, a lawyer might want to state that the client will settle a property dispute for no less than $100,000 even though client will settle for much less. A comment to Rule 4.1 states that the rule only applies to statements of fact and that some statements are not taken generally to be statements of fact. The comment explains that, for example, estimates of prices on a transaction or a client's intentions as to what is a good settlement amount are ordinarily not considered statements of fact, as long as the statement is not dishonest or fraudulent.

So a lawyer may state that a client will settle for no less than $100,000 when that is not exactly true. The lawyer must, however, avoid making other statements of fact that are not true. For example, a lawyer could not ethically state that the property in question had been appraised by an independent appraiser for $300,000 if that was not true.

G. Can a Lawyer Disclose a Material Fact to Avoid Assisting a Client's Crime or Fraud?

Yes. Rule 1.2(d) states that a lawyer may not counsel or assist a client in conduct the lawyer knowns constitutes a crime or fraud. When a crime or fraud takes the form of a misrepresentation, Rule 4.1(b) applies because it requires a lawyer to disclose a material fact when disclosure is necessary to avoid assisting a client's crime or fraud. A lawyer acts improperly only if he or she knowingly fails to disclose. Thus, a lawyer must know of the client's criminal or fraudulent behavior for the duty to apply.

If a lawyer has knowledge of criminal or fraudulent behavior, the lawyer should consider all other methods to terminate the client's criminal acts short of disclosure of the confidential information. The lawyer should try to counsel the client not to pursue a criminal or fraudulent avenue. If this approach is unsuccessful, the lawyer may have to withdraw to avoid involvement in the crime or fraud. If the lawyer's involvement is such that continuing to represent the client is continuing to assist the crime or fraud, Rule 1.16(a) demands withdrawal. If third parties are continuing to rely on the lawyer's past work touching upon the crime or fraud, the lawyer also must give notice to third parties that the withdrawal has occurred. In such a situation, a lawyer might have to disavow documents she prepared.

Finally, if withdrawal does not put the necessary distance between the lawyer and the client's criminal or fraudulent acts, the lawyer must disclose whatever material facts are necessary so that the lawyer does not assist the client in the illegal activities. Rule 4.1(b) limits this duty by requiring disclosure only when Rule 1.6 does not prohibit such a disclosure. However, Rule 1.6 permits disclosure in many situations. If the client is using the lawyer's services in furtherance of a crime or fraud reasonably certain to result in substantial financial or property injury, Rule 1.6(b) permits disclosure to prevent the client's crime or fraud. If the client has used the lawyer's services in furtherance of a crime or fraud reasonably certain to result in financial or property injury, Rule 1.6(b) permits disclosure to prevent the injury. And in the rare situation where the lawyer reasonably believes there is danger of reasonably certain death or substantial bodily harm, Rule 1.6(b) allows a lawyer to disclose information necessary to prevent the injury.

H. Does a Lawyer Have a Duty of Honesty to the Court?

Yes, most definitely. In fact, this duty of candor to the tribunal trumps most other duties a lawyer has, including, sometimes, the duty of the lawyer to the client. The duty of candor to the court is based upon the premise that the judicial system cannot perform properly if the other players in the system cannot trust the lawyers. Rule 3.3 has specific requirements of utmost candor when the lawyer deals with the tribunal.

A tribunal is a court or other body acting in an adjudicative capacity, so this duty applies in any situation in which a body will render a binding legal judgement affecting a party's interests in a particular matter. Whenever a lawyer deals with an entity like this, the lawyer must act with candor as required by Rule 3.3.

Rule 3.3 provides that when dealing with a tribunal, a lawyer may not knowingly make an untrue statement of fact or law. The tribunal must be able to trust what a lawyer says so the lawyer must speak truthfully, even about small matters. Occasionally a lawyer makes an untrue statement to the court about a matter. Perhaps a lawyer on appeal knowingly tells the court that the lower court made certain findings when in fact the court did not. Or perhaps the lawyer tells the court that certain matters were discussed below when in fact the issues were not discussed at all. Perhaps the lawyer states the facts of the matter in the brief with so much spin that the recitation of facts is false. In each of these situations, the lawyer has violated Rule 3.3.

In addition, a lawyer violates Rule 3.3 by a failure to disclose information. The rules consider a failure to disclose to be the equivalent of an affirmative misrepresentation. Lawyers must be truthful about the law as well. Occasionally, lawyers intentionally modify quotes from cases to make the precedent seem more favorable to their client. For example, what if ellipses are used to convert a sentence found in a case to a sentence having quite a different meaning? When a lawyer does something like this knowingly, the lawyer is making a false statement about the law in violation of Rule 3.3(a). When the court discovers such conduct, the court may report the lawyer to the disciplinary authorities. This conduct is considered a very serious violation.

In addition to the duty to avoid making false statements of fact or law, a lawyer must correct any untrue statement of material fact or law made to the court by the lawyer. If a lawyer states at appellate argument that a witness testified to a certain fact, but the lawyer later learns that she was mistaken about the testimony, the lawyer has a duty to correct the misimpression as long as the proceeding has not concluded. A proceeding has concluded when a final judgment has been affirmed on appeal or the time for appeal has expired. Rule 3.3 notes that this duty to correct a false statement may require disclosure of information concerning which the lawyer otherwise owes the client a duty of confidentiality under Rule 1.6. In other words, the lawyer's duty to the court trumps the lawyer's duty to the client to protect confidences.

What about legal authority? Rule 3.3 requires a lawyer to disclose to the tribunal legal authority in the controlling jurisdiction known to the lawyer to be directly adverse to the position of the client and not disclosed by opposing counsel. The rationale of the rule is that the failure to disclose legal authority to the tribunal simply leads to unneeded expenditure of judicial resources because judges and their staffs must research matters anew. If a court does not uncover a relevant precedent, the dangers are that a superior court will reverse the lawyer's court's decision, or the decision, based on an incomplete picture of relevant precedent, will create inconsistent precedent. The ultimate result will be a waste of resources.

There are a few exceptions to this duty to disclose adverse legal authority. First, Rule 3.3(a) is written so that only a knowing failure to disclose is a violation. So if a lawyer is simply a poor researcher and does not find the case that is directly adverse, the lawyer may be incompetent and liable for malpractice, but the lawyer has not violated Rule 3.3. Because of the material statement requirement, it is very difficult to prove that the lawyer has knowingly failed to disclose authority to a tribunal. Such proof is possible, however. A second qualifier is that a lawyer need not disclose the legal authority unless that authority is "directly adverse." While one can often argue that a particular legal authority is directly adverse, courts often view this as a requirement to disclose authority of which a court would want to be aware before making a decision in the matter.

A third point is that the lawyer need only disclose the authority if it is from the controlling jurisdiction. A case directly on point in a neighboring state is not one that must disclosed. Finally, there is no need to disclose if opposing counsel discloses the legal authority. One would think that the opposing counsel would want to rely on a case that is directly adverse to the lawyer's position and is from the controlling jurisdiction. So really the duty to disclose adverse authority only arises when the opposing counsel fails to identify the case.

Even if a lawyer must disclose legal authority under Rule 3.3, the lawyer is free to distinguish it, critique it, or otherwise ignore it, as long as it is cited to the court. The duty to disclose continues until the judgment has been affirmed or the time for appeal has passed.

I.   What if the Lawyer Knows a Witness Is Going to Offer False Evidence?

Lawyers are officers of the court and this role places limits on their representation of clients. If a lawyer knows that a witness will testify falsely or that other evidence is false, the lawyer may not offer that witness or evidence. Rule 3.3(a) prohibits the offering of evidence the lawyer knows to be false. This prohibition applies not only to the presentation of evidence at trial but also in depositions or any other proceeding conducted under the court's powers. For example, a lawyer cannot offer a document that the lawyer knows is fraudulent as evidence even though the client demands that the lawyer do so. The MPRE likes to test this issue— an MPRE question will present the improper conduct, but will make it seem proper because the client requested the conduct. The fact that the client demands the conduct does not absolve the lawyer of the duty of candor to the tribunal.

The lawyer should try to convince the client that the proposed conduct is inappropriate. But if the effort fails and the lawyer knows that a witness plans to lie on the stand, the lawyer cannot put that witness on the stand. Of course, it is very hard to know definitively what a person will do—remember that the standard is that a lawyer must *know* of the false testimony.

In a criminal case, this issue is more complex. The rules prohibit the lawyer's presentation of false evidence, but the criminal defendant has a constitutional right to testify. However, the criminal defendant has no constitutional right to testify falsely. Courts generally require that a lawyer allow a criminal defendant to testify even if the lawyer knows that the client will testify falsely. The lawyer must follow any local court rules for such situations, but generally courts require the lawyer to put the criminal defendant on the stand. The lawyer may assist the client in eliciting truthful testimony and then leave the defendant to testify in a narrative fashion about the matters about which the lawyer believes the client will testify falsely. To do so, the lawyer will ask an open-ended question such as: "Do you have something to share with the court today?" The lawyer cannot ask specific questions and the lawyer also cannot rely on the false testimony in any closing argument or in further questioning of other witnesses. When completed in that fashion, the lawyer does not participate in the presentation of false testimony.

In these types of circumstances, it is quite possible that a conflict between the lawyer and the client over the lawyer's inability to present evidence causes the relationship to break down. The client may want a new lawyer. If so, Rule 1.16 requires a lawyer to request permission from the court to be removed as counsel of record and, if the court grants the request, the lawyer must take all other necessary steps for withdrawal from the representation. A lawyer may not disclose confidential information in seeking permission to withdraw if the disclosure is not otherwise permitted by Rule 3.3 or another rule. Unfortunately, the conflict may not occur until the trial is actually going on. The court may not allow the lawyer to withdraw at that point, but a lawyer does not violate the rules by following the direction of the court.

J. What Happens if the Lawyer Discovers False Evidence After It Was Presented to the Court?

If the lawyer discovers later that material but false evidence was presented to the court, Rule 3.3 provides that the lawyer take reasonable remedial measures. The same is true if the lawyer later learns that her client has testified falsely or if a witness called by the lawyer has testified falsely. The false evidence need not have been elicited by the lawyer. The lawyer is responsible for any witness he or she puts on the stand. Note that this duty of the lawyer to take remedial measures is only if the false evidence is *material*.

K. Are Prosecutors Limited About What They Can Say About a Case?

Yes, prosecutors are held to a higher standard than other lawyers with regard to discouraging potential prejudicial comments, and they have additional duties and restrictions on their speech under Rule 3.8. This is a favorite topic in the MPRE, so take note if you see a fact pattern specifically involving a prosecutor. Rule 3.8 prohibits a prosecutor from making extrajudicial comments that have a substantial likelihood of heightening public condemnation of the accused. Rule 3.8 does allow prosecutors to make statements necessary to inform the public of the nature and extent of the prosecutor's action and that serve a legitimate law enforcement purpose. A prosecutor further must take care to prevent people associated with or employed by the prosecutor from making any statement that Rule 3.8 forbids the prosecutor from making. For example, a prosecutor must caution the police and other associates with whom the prosecutor works not to make inappropriate public statements.

L. What Kinds of Extrajudicial Statements Are Permitted?

A lawyer may state the claim involved in a matter, the offense, the defense, and the identity of the persons involved in the matter if no law specifically limits such disclosure. For example, if a juvenile is involved in a criminal matter, a statute will likely prohibit disclosure of the identity of the juvenile.

Further, a lawyer may state anything that is already a part of the public record and may comment about the scheduling of the matter and the result of any step in the progress of the matter. A lawyer may state that the matter is being investigated. A lawyer may also request assistance regarding locating evidence and information and may make a statement that warns the public or a particular individual of harm if the lawyer has reasonable to believe there is a likelihood of substantial harm to an individual or the public interest.

If the matter is criminal, the lawyer may make the statements discussed above, and in addition, may state that an arrest has been made and the time and place of the arrest. The lawyer may state the identity of the accused as well as the accused's residence, the accused's occupation, and the accused's family status. The lawyer may identify the investigating officer or agency. The lawyer may state how long the investigation has been ongoing as well. The lawyer may make a public statement containing information necessary to assist in the apprehension of the accused if the accused has not yet been apprehended. This portion of Rule 3.6 is of particular importance to prosecutors.

Finally, lawyers can make replies to public statements made by another attorney. Perhaps in a criminal matter the police have made statements to the press that have placed a lawyer's client in a bad light. Rule 3.6(c) provides that a lawyer may make statements otherwise not permitted by Rule 3.6 if a reasonable lawyer would believe that the response is needed to lessen the substantial undue prejudicial effect created by the statements of others. The lawyer's responsive comment, however, must state only what is necessary to mitigate the effects of the earlier statements of others.

CHAPTER 15

Termination of the Attorney-Client Relationship

Most legal representations occur because a client asks a lawyer for representation. Lawyers do have freedom in such situations to accept the representation or not. An attorney-client relationship exists when a person reasonably believes that a lawyer represents that person. However, there are certain situations when a lawyer may not allow a representation to occur, and there are other situations in which a lawyer may act to terminate a relationship. This chapter will cover both issues.

A. When *Must* an Attorney-Client Relationship End?

Rule 1.16 governs the termination of an attorney-client relationship, and there are three situations in which a lawyer either cannot accept a representation or must withdraw. Rule 1.16(a) provides that a lawyer may not accept a representation if to do so would violate law or the Rules of Professional Responsibility for the lawyer. For example, let's say a lawyer realized that accepting a client would be an unwaivable conflict of interest under Rule 1.7. The lawyer could not take on the representation because taking on the representation would violate the conflicts provisions of the rules of professional conduct.

The second situation in which a lawyer may not accept a representation of a client is if the lawyer is not physically or mentally able to handle the matter competently. If, for example, a lawyer knows that his own mental condition would materially impair his representation of a client, the lawyer cannot accept the representation. If the lawyer already represents the client and becomes aware of a physical or mental condition that materially impairs his representation of the client, the lawyer must act to end the representation.

The third situation in which a lawyer cannot handle a representation is when the client has discharged the lawyer. This is not really an issue at the time a lawyer accepts a representation but it is an issue regarding ending a representation already in existence. The law recognizes that a client has the right to terminate a lawyer for whatever reason. The rationale for the rule is that the client must be able to rid himself of the lawyer if the client feels that the bond of trust and loyalty no longer exists between the client and the lawyer. If the client states that he wants the lawyer-client relationship to end, the lawyer must honor that wish and take steps to terminate the relationship. If a client tells the lawyer that he no longer wants the lawyer's services, the lawyer must take whatever steps are necessary in the particular representation to end his relationship with the client. These three circumstances make up the mandatory withdrawal provisions of Rule 1.16(a).

B. When *May* a Lawyer Withdraw from the Representation of a Client?

Once a lawyer agrees to represent a client, that lawyer's right to withdraw from the representation can be somewhat limited. Rule 1.16(b) deals with the issue of permissive (as opposed to mandatory) withdrawal from the representation of a client. The rule allows a lawyer to withdraw for any reason if there is no material adverse effect on the client. Here's the key: courts always look to see what, if any, prejudice will occur due to the withdrawal. Even if the withdrawal will cause a material adverse effect, the lawyer may withdraw from a representation in certain specific settings. Finally, even if the withdrawal will cause a material adverse effect, a lawyer may withdraw if other *good cause* for withdrawal exists.

First and foremost, a lawyer may withdraw for any reason if there is no material adverse effect. As long as the case is not in front of the tribunal, then the lawyer does not need permission to withdraw.

However, Rule 1.16(b) lists specific settings in which a lawyer may withdraw from a representation regardless of the adverse effect on the client. However, if the matter is already before a tribunal, the lawyer must request permission from the tribunal for the withdrawal. The tribunal might not permit the withdrawal if the client will suffer an adverse effect. Let's talk about the specific circumstances in which a lawyer may withdraw.

First, a lawyer may withdraw from a representation of a client if the client is pursuing what the lawyer believes is criminal or fraudulent conduct and the lawyer's services are involved in that conduct. Further, a lawyer may withdraw if the client has used the lawyer's services to perpetrate a crime or fraud. Maybe the lawyer has discovered that the client has been using a document prepared by the lawyer to commit fraud. Perhaps the client used the document to convince investors to invest in a scheme that is actually fraudulent, but the lawyer did not know was fraudulent at the time the lawyer performed the services. The lawyer might wish to withdraw from the representation even if the client promises to stop because now the lawyer does not trust the client. Further, if the client refuses to stop, the lawyer may be required to withdraw to avoid knowingly assisting a crime or fraud. Remember that knowingly assisting a crime or fraud would violate Rule 1.2(d), the Scope of Representation, between lawyer and client. Thus, the mandatory withdrawal provision of Rule 1.16(a) would require withdrawal.

Even if the lawyer is not required to withdraw, the lawyer could choose to withdraw on the basis that the lawyer reasonably believes the client will continue to pursue a path of fraudulent conduct involving the lawyer's services.

Second, a lawyer may withdraw from a representation if the client insists on actions with which the lawyer fundamentally disagrees or considers "repugnant." Usually, a lawyer becomes aware of these sorts of issues before the representation begins and can simply decline the representation. Occasionally, though, the lawyer is already in the process of the representation before discovering the client's plan and the lawyer's disagreement with it. For example, the lawyer may have agreed to represent the client in a litigation matter. Only after discovery is in progress does the lawyer realize that the client intends to abuse the discovery process by delaying the disclosure of documents clearly subject to discovery. The lawyer may withdraw because he does not want to be a part of this type of conduct.

Third, a lawyer may withdraw from a representation if the client fails to fulfill an obligation owed to the lawyer. Rule

1.16(b)(5) is the provision of the rules that contains this permissive withdrawal situation, and it is loaded with qualifiers. First, the client must fail substantially to fulfill an obligation to the lawyer. Second, the obligation must relate to the lawyer's services. Third, the lawyer must first give the client warning that the lawyer is considering withdrawal if the client fails to fulfill the obligation.

The most obvious example of an unfilled obligation is the client's failure to pay the lawyer as the client has agreed to do in the attorney-client engagement. If the lawyer has billed the client thousands of dollars, and the client has not paid, the lawyer may withdraw. If the client pays a part of the amount due, then the lawyer must evaluate whether the client has failed "substantially" to fulfill his obligation to the lawyer. The lawyer may not withdraw unless there has been a substantial failure to fulfill an obligation.

Fourth, a lawyer may withdraw from a representation if continuing the representation causes an unreasonable financial burden on the lawyer. If a client does not pay the lawyer and the representation is continuing to require a large amount of the lawyer's time, the lawyer must invest more and more in the client's representation. There may come a point at which it is unreasonable for the lawyer to be required to shoulder the continued expense of the representation.

Fifth, a lawyer may also withdraw if the client has made the representation unreasonably difficult. Perhaps the client has retained the lawyer to handle the negotiation for the sale of a business. After a time, the client no longer communicates to the lawyer about conversations with the potential purchaser, or does not inform the lawyer of meeting dates with a potential purchaser, or generally ignores the lawyer. The lawyer could withdraw from the representation because the client has made the representation unreasonably difficult, if not impossible.

Finally, Rule 1.16(b) concludes with a final situation of permissive withdrawal: a lawyer may withdraw when "other good cause" exists, as long as the withdrawal does not prejudice the client's case.

C. When Does the Court Have to Agree to the Withdrawal?

A lawyer representing a client in a matter that does not involve a tribunal may terminate a representation by notifying the client that the lawyer will no longer be representing the client after a stated reasonable period of time. In contrast, if a lawyer represents a client in a matter that involves a tribunal, the lawyer must ask the tribunal for permission to withdraw as counsel of record for the client. They court may, or may not, permit the lawyer to withdraw; the court has discretion over this issue. This is true regardless of whether the lawyer seeks to withdraw because the rules of professional conduct demand withdrawal or whether the rules simply allow the lawyer to withdraw.

Moving for permission can sometimes be difficult to accomplish because the lawyer must not improperly disclose confidential information protected by Rule 1.6. Respecting this duty means that the lawyer may not be able to fully explain to the court the reason the lawyer is requesting permission to withdraw. If the tribunal denies a lawyer permission to withdraw, Rule 1.16(c) requires the lawyer to continue with the representation. A lawyer is required to abide by the court's ruling and continue the representation of the client. This is true in all situations in which the tribunal's permission must be obtained for a withdrawal.

D. After Termination or Withdrawal, What Are the Lawyer's Obligations?

When a lawyer withdraws from a representation, the most important thing is to ensure that that the client is still protected. The lawyer must take, as Rule 1.16(d) states, "reasonably practicable" action to protect the client. The lawyer must give the client reasonable notice of the withdrawal so that the client may act to obtain replacement counsel. The lawyer must return all the property of the client that the lawyer may have, such as any unearned advance fees or advances on expenses not yet incurred. The lawyer must give the client papers to which the client is entitled. The lawyer may retain papers only to the extent permitted by other law. The lawyer must take any other action necessary to protect the client's interests if that action is reasonably practicable.

One question that often arises in a withdrawal situation is exactly how the lawyer must treat the client's file in the lawyer's possession. Items in the lawyer's file that the client gave to the lawyer to assist in the representation are the property of the client and must be returned. With regard to all else, the rules do not provide much guidance. Typically, a lawyer should allow clients to have copies of everything in the lawyer's file and should provide the file promptly after the representation ends.

In sum, the key to withdrawal in any situation is that the client is protected. If the case has proceeded in front of a tribunal, then the lawyer must receive the court's permission prior to withdrawal.